☞ W9-CNY-055

LABOR RELATIONS AND PUBLIC POLICY SERIES

NO. 16

AN ADMINISTRATIVE APPRAISAL
OF THE NLRB

(Revised Edition)

by

EDWARD B. MILLER

UNIVERSITY OF PENNSYLVANIA

The Wharton School

INDUSTRIAL RESEARCH UNIT

LABOR RELATIONS AND PUBLIC POLICY SERIES

NO. 16

AN ADMINISTRATIVE APPRAISAL OF THE NLRB

(Revised Edition)

by

EDWARD B. MILLER
Former Chairman of the NLRB

INDUSTRIAL RESEARCH UNIT
The Wharton School, Vance Hall/CS
University of Pennsylvania
Philadelphia, Pennsylvania 19104
U.S.A.

Foreword

During his tenure as chairman of the National Labor Relations Board, Edward B. Miller devoted considerable time and energy in attempting to improve the procedures of the Board and to hasten its decision-making process. Impressed by his work as Board chairman, his judicious opinions, and his knowledge of the practical problems in the labor relations field, I remarked to him at a meeting at which he spoke in late 1974 that after he retired I would like to interest him in doing a monograph on the Board's administrative process. He indicated interest, but declined to discuss it until his retirement.

After that retirement took place, I contacted him again; and in the course of several discussions, he agreed in March 1975 to take on the project as a monograph in our Labor Relations and Public Policy Series. This series had been inaugurated in 1968 as a means of examining issues and stimulating discussions in the complex and controversial areas of collective bargaining and the regulation of labor-management disputes. Of the fifteen studies published since then, nine have dealt with various aspects of the National Labor Relations Board's administration and interpretation of the National Labor Relations (Taft-Hartley) Act. It therefore seemed altogether fitting that we should contract with Mr. Miller to write a monograph concerning the administration of the Board and that we should publish the results of this concern in our Labor Relations and Public Policy Series. The work was originally to be completed and published in 1976, but was held up by litigation in which the author was involved and by the procrastination of his former agency in supplying requested information.

Actually, Mr. Miller has done much more than that for which we contracted. He has written an essay describing informally and understandably how the National Labor Relations Board works in practice. His book is an excellent introduction to the Act, how it works, and how it affects companies, unions, and individuals. Practitioners or students who desire greater understanding of the fine points of the law can turn to other studies in our Labor Relations and Public Policy Series. For example, after reading of the Board as an "honest ballot association," (chapters I, II, and IV), one should then examine *The NLRB and the Appropriate Bargaining Unit* by John E. Abodeely and *NLRB Regulation of Election Conduct* by Robert E. Williams, Peter A. Janus, and Kenneth C. Huhn. Then after reading Mr. Miller's description of the Board as a "public law enforcer" (chapters I, III, V, and VIII), the reader should examine *The NLRB and Secondary Boycotts* by Ralph M. Dereshinsky, *The NLRB and Management Decision Making* by Robert A. Swift, *NLRB and Judicial Control of Union Discipline* by Thomas J. Keeline, and *Compulsory Unionism, the NLRB, and the Courts* by Thomas R. Haggard. This complementary reading will provide a thorough analysis of the handling of unfair labor practices and of a multitude of problems associated therewith.

Beyond this introduction to how the Board works in practice, Mr. Miller has provided an extraordinarily incisive analysis of procedural problems. In so doing, he has also shown why the so-called labor reform bill, passed by the House of Representatives in October 1977, would not have solved these problems but would have actually multiplied them. No one prior to Mr. Miller has so carefully analyzed the key role of the administrative law judges ("trial examiners" until the nomenclature was changed) and the problems involved in obtaining both good judges and hardworking judges. As he documents, this key road block to administrative progress cannot be effectively removed unless, first, the dead hand of the Civil Service Commission is removed from the selection of judges, and, second, procedures are instituted to have the judges perform a much more efficient and effective job.

The legislation enacted by the House of Representatives would have added two more members to the five-man Board. This also would not have accomplished its purpose, according to Mr. Miller, if the goal is to speed up processes and not just to insure a clear majority of appointments favorable to the administration in power. Mr. Miller points out that each Board member has a large staff, that these staffs work independently, and that the net effect of two more Board members would be to add two more independent bureaucracies vying with each other and not necessarily accomplishing improvements in Board procedures.

Finally, as Mr. Miller points out, neither the expedited elections nor the heavy penalties provided for in that legislation would have accomplished the purpose envisioned. The heavy penalties surely were severe, but it is likely that they would have trapped small companies rather than intimidated large concerns that have sophisticated legal advice; thus, the measures would have forced employees into unions which they did not choose.

The requirement for elections within a certain time would obviously cause employers to alter their tactics by refusing to agree to consent elections which have been, up to now, one of the most successful aspects of NLRB procedure.

At the request of the Industrial Research Unit, Mr. Miller has revised this work, making several minor corrections, including a new Table 15, which more accurately reflects the appellate work done by the Enforcement Litigation staff. Although the proposed "labor reform" bill was stopped by a filibuster in the Senate, the discussion of its provisions is still a clear analysis of what should be avoided in Taft-Hartley amendments.

I believe that this book should be widely read both by students and legislators. It points the way to improved administration by carefully analyzing practice. Its commonsense approach is especially valuable to those who have failed to probe beneath NLRB procedure and action; and it raises questions about "reforms" and other mechanisms which appear to have been designed without thorough understanding of how the processes which do exist actually work in practice or where the problems really rest.

*   *   *

The manuscript was edited by Mr. Robert E. Bolick, Jr., assisted by Mrs. Karen M. Rose and Miss Maria S. Stathis. Mrs. Margaret E. Doyle handled the administrative matters associated with the project. The research and cost of publication were financed in part by a grant from the Weyerhauser Company and largely from the generous grants of the Pew Memorial Trust in support of the Labor Relations and Public Policy Series. The author is, of course, solely responsible for the research and for the views expressed, which should in no way be attributed to the grantor, to the author's law firm or associates, or to the University of Pennsylvania.

HERBERT R. NORTHRUP, *Director*
Industrial Research Unit
The Wharton School

Philadelphia
August 1978

TABLE OF CONTENTS

LIST OF TABLES

CHAPTER I

The National Labor Relations Board — What Is It?

The National Labor Relations Board plays two important, but limited roles: (1) it is an honest ballot association; and (2) it is a public law enforcer.

THE HONEST BALLOT ASSOCIATION

As an honest ballot association, it sets up and runs elections. These are the now commonplace employee elections in which the employees decide by secret ballot vote whether they want to be represented by a union and, if so, by which one. If a majority of those voting choose union representation, then by law, the union is the exclusive agent for every employee in the voting unit (whether he or she casts a ballot or not, and no matter which way he or she voted) in all dealings with the employer concerning virtually all matters affecting wages, hours, and working conditions.

Such an election usually results from a petition filed with the NLRB by a union which seeks to demonstrate its majority status and thus gain governmentally sanctioned and legally enforceable bargaining rights. Sometimes, however, such an election is held because employees who already have union representation have filed a petition for an election to oust the union which has been representing them. An election may also result from a petition filed by an employer who may be confronted with a demand for recognition by a union (or conflicting demands by rival unions) and who is unwilling to grant recognition without governmentally certified proof of majority status.

The Board has developed guidelines for the circumstances under which it will grant a petition for election submitted to it by a union, by employees, or by an employer. We will not probe those guidelines in any depth in this book because we are not here attempting to provide an evaluation of the law, but rather to outline what the Board does and to evaluate in some measure how efficiently it performs the tasks with which it is charged. The reader will want, however, some notion of the nature of the tasks, so we shall include, here and elsewhere, some general outline of the substance of the Board's work.

The Board's rules about when it will and when it will not hold an election are, in general, designed either to implement the intent of the law and its purposes as perceived by the Board, or simply to ease administration. Some rules evidence both considerations.

For example, the Board will not hold an election during the life of a collective bargaining contract of reasonable duration (not over three years). That rule has its roots in considerations of industrial relations stability. Effective collective bargaining, says the Board, cannot work if established relationships are allowed to be disrupted at frequent and unpredictable times.

Nor will the Board conduct an election if only a very small group of employees seem to want one. A 30 percent "showing of interest" is required. That is an administrative, rather than a public policy, rule, designed to save the Board the time and expense of holding an election when there is not enough employee interest to suggest that the election has any practical chance of resulting in a change in the *status quo*.

The Board also will not conduct an employer-sought election if no reasonable objective basis can be shown for doubting the continuing majority status of an incumbent union. This rule combines practical and policy reasons. As a policy matter, the Board does not want to be a party to a mere delaying game designed solely to stall an employer's bargaining obligations for a while. In addition, it is in the interest of ease of administration not to hold obviously futile elections.

Because these and dozens of other rules have been tested out in factual situations, they have become rather intricate. The criticism is sometimes made that they have become so complex as to be difficult to comprehend. Yet in administering any law, borderline cases do come along. In deciding a considerable number and variety of those borderline cases, rules do become meticulously refined. The total of those refinements becomes a set of rules which may seem forbidding to a newcomer to the process. Yet the same process of developing detailed rules seems to have eventuated in administering and interpreting every other law. And, for that matter, it seems also to result in similarly detailed rules in baseball, football, bridge, and virtually every other set of our attempts, for pleasure or for business, to structure human relationships.

As a part of running elections, one of the functions, then, of an honest ballot association is to make rules and to apply and enforce them. Such rules involve not only when and if to run an election, but also determinations of what kinds of employee groups are "appropriate" for bargaining and hence for the holding of an election; which employees are eligible to vote; and, once the votes have all been cast, whether the election is valid or invalid. Was it properly run by the NLRB? Did one party or another conduct itself, either at the polls or in the course of the election campaign, in a manner which so tainted the atmosphere of the election as to make the results unreliable?

The Board's role as an honest ballot association thus involves not only administering the mechanics of balloting, but also a substantial area of administrative supervision, rulemaking, and deciding disputes over whether its rules have been violated. In a subsequent chapter, we will examine in some further detail the means by which these various administrative and quasi-judicial functions are carried out, and will, in yet another chapter, attempt to evaluate how well they are administered.

THE PUBLIC LAW ENFORCER

The Board's second role is as a public law enforcer. Each one of the three words in that title embodies an important concept.

The Board is a PUBLIC law enforcer. With but a few exceptions, only the Board can enforce this law. Unions cannot. Employers cannot. Employees cannot. A union cannot go into court and file a lawsuit against an employer, complaining that the employer has committed "unfair labor practices." An employee cannot go into court and do that either. An employer faced with illegal recognition picketing cannot go to court to enjoin that picketing or to seek damages caused by it. When the National Labor Relations Act was passed, the concept was that there should be a *public* enforcer, not a rash of individually brought lawsuits seeking to enforce private rights and resulting in cluttering the courts with a mass of litigation over labor disputes.

That basic concept has continued, but some exceptions have been engrafted on to the law as the NLRA has been amended. Employers *can* now sue unions for damages for certain prohibited secondary boycotts. An individual employee *can* now sue a union in a private suit, if that union has failed to represent him fairly. A union *can* sue an employer for breach of a collective bargaining contract. Despite these exceptions, however, the National Labor Relations Act continues to be primarily enforced by and through the National Labor Relations Board.

In retrospect, the concept of public prosecution appears to have been a sound one. It has prevented harrassment of parties by groundless lawsuits, while at the same time insuring that law violations do not go undetected and unremedied because an injured party may not have either the resources or the will to maintain a private suit. Companies and unions have come to have respect for this law because they know a public prosecutor will pursue alleged violations through litigation if voluntary compliance does not occur.

We have said that the NLRB is a public LAW enforcer. It does not and cannot enforce anything but the *law*. This does not always seem widely understood. Many people seem to expect the Board to formulate and administer abstract justice in the labor relations field. Some seem to envision the Board as a governmentally sponsored Robin Hood with a mission of aiding the weak and restraining the strong. With some frequency, one hears the complaint that the Board does not stop big unions from forcing small, weak employers into paying highly inflationary wage rates; or that the Board will not help employees, even though their employer has forced them to work unduly long hours or under onerous conditions; or that it has not helped some small union which seems unable to win elections among employees in a major company whose lawfully conducted election campaigns are regularly successful in persuading employees to vote against union representation.

Still others see the Board in the role of the public's representative in bargaining and ask why it has not prevented inflationary settlements or settled lengthy strikes which are disruptive of the nation's economy.

In fact, the Board has authority to do none of those things. It has only the narrow authority to be an enforcer of the *law* which gave rise to its existence.

The Congress has written, and twice substantially amended, the National Labor Relations Act. It is to those enactments and only to those enactments that one must look to find the boundaries of the Board's enforcement authority. Only where conduct of unions or employers is prohibited by the Act does the Board have any authority to enter the picture. It is a public law enforcer—not a public policy setter in morals, economics, the conduct of internal union affairs, or the development of employer personnel practices.

Thirdly, the NLRB is a public law ENFORCER. Within its own structure, this agency has a variety of interwoven processes by which it makes tentative determinations of whether the law has been violated. It has, however, no authority either to make final determinations of guilt or innocence, nor to remedy any violations which are tentatively found by it to have taken place. No order of this agency has any force or effect until a *court* concurs with the Board's findings and gives court sanction to a remedial order recommended by the Board.

Some other federal and state agencies have administrative enforcement tools, such as the right to grant and revoke licenses. The NLRB has none. Nor does a violation of the law administered by this agency give rise to any criminal liability.

Thus, if the Board finds that an unfair labor practice has been committed, it can enter an order designed to remedy the unfair labor practice. But if the respondent union or employer does not heed its order, then the Board must go to a court of appeals and try to persuade that court that its (the Board's) order is worthy of enforcement under all of the circumstances. If the court agrees and "enforces" the Board order, but the violation continues or remains unremedied, then and then only has the offending employer or union truly run afoul of the law, in which instance civil or criminal contempt penalties may be invoked.

Because the agency has been so settlement-minded and because a large measure of voluntary compliance has been achieved, this basic lack of agency authority sometimes tends to be forgotten. Yet it is an important factor in the law's administration.

So we see that the Board's role when the law is violated is PUBLIC, has its roots only in the LAW, and must be affirmatively ENFORCED in a court by the Board.

CHAPTER II

The Honest Ballot Association and How It Functions

In chapter I, we described briefly the Board's role as an honest ballot association. We turn now to a closer look at how that function is carried out, at what its basic administrative segments are, and at when, where, and by whom they are performed.

WHEN THE PARTIES WANT A TELLER

The Board's election cases are begun when representatives of a union, of a group of employees, or of an employer file a petition for an election. When that election petition is filed, the Board's first act is to notify all interested parties. Thus, if a union files a petition seeking an election in an unorganized plant, the employer is promptly notified. Or, if an employer or group of employees file a petition to oust a union as the bargaining agent, the union is promptly notified. The reason for the notification is more than courtesy or legal formality. The Board wants to know promptly whether it can get the agreement of the other party to hold an election.

In a very substantial number of cases—76 percent in 1974 and 73 percent in 1975, for example—the other party has shown itself willing to cooperate,[1] and the details of the election are worked out by voluntary agreement of the parties with the aid and assistance of a Board agent. Such agreements can be reduced to writing and executed in the course of a Board-arranged conference, often within a matter of an hour or two or, in the case of very large elections, perhaps a day or two. In these cases, the parties primarily want a teller. They want the election run correctly; they want proper notices of the election to be posted; they want the ballots counted by an impartial observer; they want somebody to supervise the polling; and they

---

[1] 39 NLRB ANN. REP. 200 (1974) ; 40 NLRB ANN. REP. 209 (1975).

want a proper certificate of the result. The Board performs all those jobs very well, as it should, having accumulated over forty years of experience in doing them.

The Tellers' Duties

To assist the parties in reaching these agreements, Board agents will be found in many places—on the premises of employers in remote country towns, in heavily industrialized segments of our cities, or aboard ships in harbors—and at virtually every hour of the day or night.

Even in the simplest of elections, there are many details to be tended to. Anyone who has been asked to conduct an election of officers in his own club or church knows that careful attention to election details takes time, effort, and good planning.

Basics include suitable agreements about when and where the election will take place. Most employers are willing to permit an NLRB election to be held in a convenient location in the plant. Dates and times of day for the election are selected under the supervision of the Board and in a manner designed to afford the employees a convenient time to vote, while at the same time enabling the election to be conducted as efficiently as possible; for example, polling times are set to encompass the end of one shift and the beginning of another.

Printed notices, designed to be impartial and to advise employees of both the details of the election and of their rights under the law, are prepared and sent out to the locations involved for posting several days in advance of the election. Ballots must be printed—sometimes in one or more foreign languages if there are a number of voters whose knowledge of English is limited. Election observers from both the union and the company must be instructed in their duties.

The utmost care must be taken to preserve the secrecy of the ballot, which means that suitable polling areas must be arranged for. Municipal voting booths may have to be borrowed, or portable booths may have to be brought out to the election site by the Board agent. Ballot boxes which can be properly sealed and watched must be provided and brought to the election. Properly prepared ballots must also be ready in time for the election. (It strikes terror in the hearts of Board agents to think they might someday through oversight show up for an election without the ballots! It has happened, but very rarely.) Polls must be supervised tactfully but firmly so that the voting can take place in an orderly and dignified manner. Proper announcements of the election may sometimes be made over the plant's loudspeaker system, usually by a Board agent. If there is a problem of releasing voters from work, suitable arrangements must be made and supervised by Board agents so that employees receive clear and timely notice of their right to leave their work stations to mark and deposit their ballots.

Ultimately, the ballots must be counted; and, if no objections are filed within the time period provided in the Board's rules, a properly worded certificate of the election's outcome must be issued.

Thus, even though in many cases, the parties primarily want a teller, there are a host of duties to be performed, ranging from simple clerical functions to considerable feats of diplomacy in arranging things to the satisfaction of all parties concerned so that time-consuming formal proceedings can be avoided.

In many respects, the holding of these elections is the most important function the Board performs. Thus, although perhaps not the most glamorous or exciting function performed by Board personnel, the administration of these elections is nevertheless of vital significance to unions, employees, and employers. That the Board has been able to administer this segment of its operations in a manner which is rarely criticized speaks well for the ability of its administrators over the years.

WHEN THERE IS A "UNIT" FIGHT—OR, WHEN SOMEBODY WANTS TO PLAY FOR DELAY

The parties do not always want just a teller. There are sometimes real controversies over whether there should be an election at all, over what "unit," if any, is "appropriate" for the holding of an election, and over who is eligible to vote. Is John Doe a "supervisor" and thus ineligible to vote, or is he merely a "leadman"—a more experienced craftsman to whom employees look for guidance, but who has no true supervisory duties and is thus eligible to vote? Does Jane Doe work with sufficient regularity to be a "regular part-timer" and thus eligible to vote, or does she work so sporadically as to be deemed a "casual" employee without a continuing interest in terms and conditions of employment and thus ineligible to vote?

Some questions of eligibility can be postponed until after the election. Thus, if John shows up at the polls, he may vote;

but his ballot may be challenged by whatever party believes him ineligible. If his vote is necessary to determine the outcome of the election, the eligibility issue can be decided then; if his vote is not determinative, then it will not be necessary to resolve the challenge. But that procedure is followed only when the number of such voters is fairly small and will not unduly prolong the postelection procedures.

Furthermore, serious questions about the size and shape of the unit are more basic than mere voter eligibility and are not deferrable. Questions such as whether the group is appropriate at all for an election must sometimes be resolved. For example, should an election be held in just one plant of an employer, or are the employer's three plants so interdependent and so integrated that only a unit comprised of all three plants is an appropriate one in which to hold an election? Is there a contract in effect which "bars" an election until near its expiration? Or does the contract claimed to be a bar not really cover this unit of employees? Is it defective as a bar because it contains illegal provisions?

Regional Directors and Decision Making

Although not providing a complete measure of the scope of issues which may arise, the above are examples of disputes which may not prove resolvable in the conference room by agreement of the parties. When agreement is not reached, a hearing must be held and the decision-making process invoked. Administratively, this means the agency must provide somebody to conduct a hearing and somebody to make a decision. For over half of the Board's history to date, the decision-making function in this kind of proceeding lay with the full Board in Washington, D.C. But, by an amendment to the Act in 1959, the Board was authorized to delegate substantial decision-making authority in this area to its regional directors at its discretion. It has exercised most of that discretion, and today, only very few cases of this kind reach the full Board. On his own, a regional director may transfer a case of this kind to the Board for decision if he thinks the issues are extraordinarily difficult, complex, or novel. He is not, however, supposed to do so just because the record is long or the issue a little ticklish, although a few directors occasionally violate those rules to get out from under a tedious or sensitive case. In addition to such transfers, the Board reaches some cases by the "review" route. If a party believes the decision he gets from the regional director is wrong, he may, for certain quite limited reasons, request review by the Board in Washington. Such requests are filed in 25-35 percent of the cases, and the Board grants review of only about 10 percent of those requested.[2] Thus out of every 1,000 regional director decisions, only about 30 will actually be fully reviewed by the Board.

Hearings on these kinds of issues sometimes take place even though there is no genuine issue involved. Some parties refuse to sit down and work out details of a prompt election and, instead, demand a hearing merely to stall for time. There was a time that, even without agreement, the Board proceeded to an election with only a promise that it would look at the situation again after the election to see whether a hearing was really necessary. There are those who believe that that was a sound procedure. There are others who believe that, while that procedure avoided playing for delay, it also operated to deprive parties of due process because of a tendency of Board personnel to ride roughshod over genuine issues in the interest of building an administrative record for holding speedy elections. The Congress apparently was persuaded by the latter view, for the 1947 amendment to the statute vested in each party an absolute right to a hearing.

To hold hearings in "no-issue" cases may require little in the way of professional skill or brainpower from either the hearing officer or regional director. But it nevertheless requires time and often a high degree of patience on the part of Board personnel. Some counsel have been known to engage in substantial histrionics in order to give a phony issue the appearance of being a seriously contested one. In the interest of attempting to preserve a reasonably judicial image, neither the hearing officer nor the regional director can afford to deal too summarily even with contentions which may seem frivolous. The experienced "old hand" who knows the lawyers in his region and who is thoroughly knowledgeable in the field, however, can often combine expertise, common sense, and a little leavening humor in such a way as to minimize delays caused by this kind of game playing.

Whether the issues are real or contrived, one of the functions to be performed in cases where the parties are unable or un-

---

[2] Derived from NLRB ANNUAL REPORTS: *see, e.g.*, 39 NLRB ANN. REP. 200 (1974); 40 NLRB ANN. REP. 209 (1975).

willing to agree to an election is the quasi-judicial function of holding hearings and issuing written decisions. Most of the decision making in these representation cases has been taken out of Washington by the 1960 delegation of authority to the regional directors. The regions, therefore, bear the brunt of the administrative workload not only of agreed elections, but also of the decisional work which results when agreement is not reached.

AFTER THE POLL IS OVER—OR, DUE PROCESS FOR HARD LOSERS

When the voting is completed and the ballots counted, the Board's role is not necessarily over. A party may protest that the election was not valid. Or, if there are challenged ballots in sufficient numbers to affect the outcome of the election, voter eligibility questions may have to be dealt with.

Objections

Protests of the validity of the election are called "objections"; and a number of different kinds of objections may be made. For example, it may be asserted that the company or the union intimidated voters by making threats or offering bribes; or, that last minute material misrepresentations were made by one party or the other; or, that some employees were prevented from voting; or, that the Board agent conducting the election failed to keep the ballot box under close and careful observation at all times; or, that improper electioneering occurred at the polling place. It is obvious from just these few examples that a potential exists in this area for a host of disputes, and thus for further work for the agency.

An attempt is made to handle these issues without the necessity of holding a hearing on every objection. Parties making objections are required to support them with documents and by tendering witnesses. If the objections are legally sufficient, if proved, to require that the election be set aside, the documents will be reviewed and the witnesses interviewed by a Board agent. It they are legally insufficient, the objections may be dismissed without any further investigation. For example, if a union objects to an election because the employer told employees he did not think unions were a good thing, no investigation will be made. Such employer comment is noncoercive "free speech" and would be legally insufficient to invalidate the election. The objection would be promptly dismissed. A similar dismissal would occur if an employer were to file an objection alleging that the union promised the employees it would negotiate a good contract for them, if elected, and that there would be big wage increases for everybody. Such forecasts of negotiating success are not regarded by the Board as improper; and thus, again, the objection could be dismissed without the need of an investigation of the allegations.

In others, however, where the incidents alleged to have occurred would, if proved, be sufficient to affect the validity of the election, a factual investigation is required. Following the investigation, a report on objections is issued to the parties. That report may recommend that the election be validated, that it be set aside, or that the investigation was inconclusive and that a hearing is necessary before there can be a proper resolution of the issues of fact and law raised by the objections.

The investigative process may or may not eliminate the need for hearing and a written decision. If a hearing and written decision are required, once again more of the workload falls on the regional offices, not on the Board in Washington. If the parties, in their preelection conference, entered into what is referred to as a "Consent Election" agreement, then the regional director has virtually the sole decision-making responsibility. If, on the other hand, a different form of agreement is used, a "Stipulation for Certification Upon Consent Election," the ultimate decision on objections, until very recently, had to be made by the full Board in Washington.[3] If the election was not the result of agreement, but was directed as a result of a hearing, then the regional director makes the decision on the objections, but the election agreement is subject to discretionary review only by the Board in Washington.

Thus, the administrative functions to be performed after the voting include an investigation, a report on objections, and possibly a hearing and formal decision. Most of the functions in this area are performed in the regional offices, with some review functions being performed by the Board in Washington.

---

[3] This kind of election agreement now gives rise only to a discretionary review by the Board in the same manner as a directed election. But because of certain assurances given to the Bar at the time this procedural change was effected, internal procedures in the Board's Washington offices had not, at the time of this writing, been altered substantially from those used for full decision making. In time, there will probably be some streamlining of the Board's method of handling these cases.

CHAPTER III

Public Law Enforcer

In this chapter, we shall examine in some further detail the nature of the functions performed within the structure of the Board in fulfilling its mission as a public law enforcer. Public law enforcement can be divided into four subfunctions: investigation, prosecution, settlement, and formal decision making. The first two of these functions and the bulk of the third are performed by the General Counsel and his attorneys and investigators. The formal decision-making function is performed exclusively by the Board and its corps of first-line decision makers, now called administrative law judges. The Board also has authority, within some limitations, to review settlements and to rule in its decision-making capacity on whether a proposed settlement should be accepted or whether it is unacceptable because it does not, in the Board's view, sufficiently remedy the alleged violation.

The separation of the Board's and General Counsel's authority and responsibility is statutorily required. The General Counsel was given independent authority in 1947 in the course of the so-called Taft-Hartley amendments. Prior to that time, he had worked hand-in-glove with the Board, both in election matters and in law enforcement matters. This appeared to many as an undesirable combination of prosecutor and judge, tending to suggest the possibility of bias on the part of the decision maker. Whatever political, legal, or philosophical arguments may be advanced for or against the desirability of this separation of functions, it did occur and has affected the nature of the administration of the agency.

WHO SAYS IT IS NOT AN UNFAIR LABOR PRACTICE?

An employee walks into the door of an NLRB regional office and says that he wants to make a complaint against his employer. Within a matter of minutes, he is referred to a lawyer or investigator who sits down with him to hear his story. The employee says that he was discharged and that, when he was given his final paycheck, the paycheck was short by $50.00. This, to the employee, is an obviously unfair labor practice, and he seeks relief. He will be told promptly and firmly that he will get no help whatever from the National Labor Relations Board. He will also be told that he may file a formal charge if he wishes, but that, if he does so, it will have to be dismissed because the facts do not spell out a violation of the law which is administered by the National Labor Relations Board.

The unsophisticated employee is likely to be very much disappointed by this course of events. "Who says it is not an unfair labor practice?" he may be heard to mutter as he leaves the Board's office.

The answer is that the General Counsel says that it is not an unfair labor practice, and the General Counsel has very broad authority to say just that. He is, as we have pointed out earlier, a *public* prosecutor, and it is he who makes the call on whether a complaint which comes to his attention has "merit"— *i.e.*, arguably appears to make out a violation of the prohibitions of the Act which are referred to in the Act's terminology as "unfair labor practices." Those prohibitions obviously do not encompass everything "unfair" which either a union or an employer may do; they encompass only those things which the Act, by its terms, makes "unfair." The General Counsel and his staff screen the thousands of verbal and written complaints which come into the Board's offices each year to determine whether the conduct complained of by the individual, the employer, or the union is such that, if proved, a violation of the law has occurred which requires remedying.

If he makes a determination that there may be a violation of the law worthy of prosecution, it then becomes necessary to investigate the facts which the charging party says took place. First, a form called a "charge" must be signed by the charging party, and it forms the foundation for the beginning of a file on the case. An investigator must then be assigned to check out the facts. After the facts have been dug out and reviewed, the regional director must make a determination of whether there is sufficient merit to proceed further. The technique by which such determinations are arrived at will vary from region to region. The procedures, which once involved sometimes extensive reports called FIRs (Field Investigation Reports), have been streamlined over the years, and oral presentations are now frequently used. Subcommittees or committees may be utilized in order to provide a broader decision-making base and also to provide for supervision and training of inexperienced investigators. Whatever the technique, the functions are the same: (1) a factual investigation, and (2) an analysis of whether such facts as appear to be provable are legally sufficient so that the public prosecutor should proceed further in an effort to remedy the violation.

Or, put more briefly, will or will not the General Counsel say that the practice in question is an unfair labor practice?

AVOID LITIGATION LIKE THE PLAGUE

The avoidance of litigation, whenever possible, is a practice long followed by the General Counsel and, fortunately, frequently followed also by those whom the General Counsel decides to accuse of violating the law.

In the fiscal year ending June 30, 1976, 34,509 charges were filed with the agency's regional offices all around the country.[1] Of these, 71.5 percent were either withdrawn or dismissed, which indicates that after investigation they were found to be without merit.[2] While General Counsels in recent years have viewed their function as being the "cutting edge of the law"— *i.e.*, willing to litigate borderline or new and novel theories of law violations so that they could be tested out through the decision-making process—nevertheless, about 70 percent of the charges were, each year, found to be either without sufficient factual support or without adequate legal justification to be worth pursuing further.[3]

There are those who say that this very large percentage of meritless charges suggests the General Counsel is wasting vast amounts of taxpayer money in investigating and discussing worthless cases. But there are two rebuttal positions to this criticism: (1) the fact that the General Counsel screens out worthless cases saves innocent respondents huge amounts of

[1] 41 NLRB ANN. REP. 4 (1976).

[2] *Id.* at 5.

[3] Derived from NLRB ANNUAL REPORTS: *see, e.g.*, 39 NLRB ANN. REP. 11 (1974).

money by shutting off worthless litigation at the very outset; and (2) the willingness of NLRB staffers to take the time patiently to investigate and discuss these charges with disgruntled employees may defuse thousands of potentially serious labor disputes each year.

Another 23 or 24 percent of the total charges filed are settled by agreement with the respondents, and only about 6 percent require a hearing.[4] Still others are settled during the hearing or immediately afterwards, and some are settled by voluntary compliance with the initial decision of the administrative law judge. Thus, the five-man Board in Washington reviews 4 percent of the total cases in which charges were initially filed during any given year.[5]

None of those settlements, dismissals or withdrawals, or instances in which compliance with a decision of the administrative law judge or the Board is achieved occur automatically. Each of them takes time, effort, and patience by regional staff personnel. Settlement of cases may be an art, but the Board's experience demonstrates that it is also a skill which can be developed. The high settlement rates which have for many years prevailed are a tribute to the efforts of the staff attorneys and investigators and to the settlement training which they consistently receive.

From an administrative point of view, this extraordinarily high settlement rate is what has kept the size of the agency within bounds and the cost to the taxpayer at least tolerable. While, as we have said, settlement efforts take time and skill, they do not take nearly the time and skill involved in the trial of a case. One hour spent in achieving a settlement saves, at a minimum, forty hours of trial and trial preparation time. If there were even a 20 or 30 percent increase in the number of cases which had to be tried each year, the cost of supporting this agency would rise astronomically. Serious attention to settlement, therefore, is essential to effective administration.

We need look only to the Equal Employment Opportunity Commission to see the results of a long-continuing failure to recognize the need for serious settlement attempts. That agency's backlog of cases continued to mount for years, while charging parties went without relief and respondents were harrassed

---

[4] *See, e.g.,* 39 NLRB ANN. REP. 210-11 (1974).

[5] *Id.*

by having to try to find facts dealing with accusations which were years old by the time the EEOC investigation began in earnest. Any lawyer practicing in the labor field knows that it was virtually impossible until fairly recently to reach a settlement within any reasonable time with the EEOC. The result was administrative chaos, harrassment of respondents, and dissatisfaction of charging parties. The total result was a failure to implement the law. The NLRB stands, in contrast, as a shining example of effective administration through settlement and deserves kudos in this regard.

MR. DISTRICT ATTORNEY

There are, however, cases which do not get settled. Over 1,500 of them have been tried in each recent year.[6] The trial of a case requires a careful investigation, including finding and analyzing needed documents, and locating and preparing witnesses to testify.

Experienced lawyers know that many hours of investigation and trial preparation are required for every hour in the courtroom or hearing room. All of this investigatory and trial work is done by field examiners and attorneys assigned to the regional offices.

The trials take place at locations convenient for the respondents and for the witnesses for the charging party—usually in the city or town where the employer's place of business is located. This means, in the larger and less populous states in particular, a considerable travel budget.

In some regions, the investigative work is performed primarily by field examiners, who are not lawyers, while in other regions, lawyers also participate extensively in both the preliminary investigation and immediate trial preparation work. At one time, some regional directors deliberately kept down the number of nonlawyers on their staffs and increased the number of lawyers so as to maintain maximum flexibility. This was, however, rather costly (attorneys' salaries being higher than those of examiners); and, under pressure from the Civil Service Commission, the NLRB within the last decade has adopted a rule of thumb of maintaining about a 50:50 ratio of lawyers to field examiners.

---

[6] *See, e.g.*, 39 NLRB ANN. REP. 199 (1974); 38 NLRB ANN. REP. 207 (1973).

The NLRB has for some years faced a problem in connection with developing and maintaining a top notch corps of trial lawyers. The primary reason for the difficulty is that law firms are able to offer, and do offer, attractive salaries to the NLRB attorney who acquires trial skill, and they can promise a future which is not subject to the same compensation limits as is government employment. Furthermore, those offers tend to go to the most competent NLRB lawyers. This means that every regional office has in its ranks only a few long-service, career government lawyers who are often forced to carry a heavy share of the trial work, even though the abilities and energy levels of many of them leave a good bit to be desired. The "cream" has very likely been skimmed off by the private firms which have lured away many of the best lawyers. There are, however, some good trial lawyers who prefer government service and who do spend their full careers with the Board. Not enough, however, fall into this category, and the General Counsel faces continuing problems of having insufficient numbers of fully qualified trial lawyers to meet the agency's prosecutory needs.

There are other deficiencies in the prosecutory staff as well. Writing skills, in particular, take very careful training and much time to develop. Most field attorneys employed by the Board do not develop these writing skills to any significant degree. Faced with the necessity of meeting deadlines and lacking some of the motivation which leads private practitioners to work long hours and on weekends to polish their written product, the writing skill of Board attorneys is often well below first class standards.

Thus, there are problems and weak spots, but the regions do keep pace with a considerable workload of investigation, preparing cases for trial, trying cases, and writing posthearing briefs to the judge as well as on appeal to the Board in unfavorable decisions. They are the Messrs. District Attorneys of the NLRB labor law field.

THE BENCH SITTERS—CALL ME JUDGE!

We have mentioned that, in election cases, the regional offices provide hearing officers, when needed, from among the regional office staff. Not so in the public law enforcer area.

When a respondent is charged with a violation of the law in a formal complaint issued by the General Counsel, the case is assigned to an administrative law judge. These first-line decision makers, until recent years called trial examiners, are not residents of the region in which the trial occurs. They are surrogates of the decision-making side of the agency—the five-man Board in Washington. For many years, all of these judges were housed in headquarters in Washington and sent out around the country to hear cases. Today, it is still true that most of the judges are located in Washington, but a West Coast office has been established, and about one-quarter of the Board's staff of administrative law judges are headquartered there, serving the western and southwestern states.

These judges are charged, first, with the responsibility of conducting the trial of unfair labor practice cases. A judge may encourage the parties to engage in settlement discussions just before opening the trial, although there is a substantial difference in attitude among the judges in this regard. Some are aggressive settlers; others make no real settlement efforts at all. The trials are conducted in much the same fashion as trials in federal courts, with perhaps some greater liberality with respect to rules of evidence.

After conducting the trial, it is the judge's responsibility to issue a written decision. The Board's administrative law judges have been accustomed to writing narrative decisions, often with rather lengthy discussions of both the facts and the law. There are some who say that much simpler and more formalistic "Findings of Fact" and "Conclusions of Law" could be used, as they are frequently in federal courts, thus consuming less paper and, more important, less of the judges' time. Others say that the requirements of the Administrative Procedures Act are such that a full discussion of the facts and the law are required. In any event, either through habit or, in some cases, to avoid the risk of having decisions upset on this point, the judges have clung to the traditional "long form" opinions. In fact, some of the judges seem to think that their opinions are going to become a part of the world's great literature. At least that conclusion follows if one looks at some of the prose styles, at some of the long essays included in the decisions, and at the length of time it takes some judges to get around to issuing their decisions!

When I was NLRB Chairman, I once referred to these first-line decision makers as "make-believe judges." In a very real sense, that is what they are. A "judge's" decision has no teeth and cannot be enforced until after the Board has reviewed and adopted it and taken it to a court of appeals to secure an enforceable order. Perhaps as a result of this dubious status and relative impotence, the Board's corps of decision makers is extraordinarily squeamish about "independence" and about titles.

The least suggestion from a member or chairman of the Board that a particular judge might do better at his task is regarded as a dangerous interference with judicial freedom. If a chief administrative law judge grows impatient and expresses displeasure with one of the corps who may be months late in getting out a decision, the chief judge and the Board members are likely to be visited by a Committee of Judges protesting that their sacred independence is being threatened.

For years these hearing officers were called trial examiners. Perhaps one of the most intensive lobbying efforts within the federal bureaucracy was carried out by trial examiners from the NLRB and from a host of other agencies in an effort to get the title changed so as to include the word "judge." In the early 1970s, the Civil Service Commission finally yielded to this lobbying pressure, and yesterday's trial examiners became today's judges. They cherish the new long-sought-after title, and some, I was told in dead seriousness, require even their own families to address them as "Judge."

In a subsequent chapter of this work, we shall deal more seriously with the administrative problems created by what may well be defensive over-sensitivity on the part of the judges. At this point, we wish primarily to identify the initial decision-making function which must be performed in determining those cases in which the Board will or will not enter an order and seek enforcement thereof.

What was probably regarded in the early days of the Board's history as merely another step in the administrative sorting process which enables the Board to determine which cases are to be seriously prosecuted in the courts has, over time, emerged as the first really *judicial* step in a three-step judicial sequence. What was once called an "Intermediate Report and Recommended Order," for example, is now called a "Judge's Decision." This change signifies, or reflects, more than just an ego massage for the former trial examiners. A change in attitude within and without the agency has really transformed the initial concept of an administrative investigation aided by a hearing into a highly structured prosecution and a very courtroom-like trial, with the parties expecting not an administrative report, but a judicial decision.

Both the Board and the Bar now regard the hearing before the administrative law judge in very much the same light as they would regard, for example, a bench trial of a Title VII case by a district court judge. It is before the administrative law judge that the basic facts of the case will be established. It is by this officer that credibility resolutions will be made, which are rarely tampered with thereafter either by the Board or by a reviewing court. In short, the case for the Board or for the respondent will essentially be won or lost in this initial unfair labor practice hearing. Thus the judges, although without so much enforceable authority as even a justice of the peace, are nevertheless regarded by the parties as performing a critical judicial, not merely an administrative, function. Their role has, no doubt, grown in importance over the years. They are more than hearing officers. They are the bench sitters and have probably earned the right to be called judge.

WHO IS TO JUDGE THE JUDGES?

Approximately 77 percent of the NLRB's administrative law judge decisions were appealed to the Board for review in 1976.[7] This compares with 75 percent in 1975 and 1970,[8] 85 percent in 1965,[9] and 86 percent in 1950.[10]

This high percentage of appeals is probably due to the fact that an appeal buys time. We have already commented on the fact that the judges' decisions have no real teeth. There is, therefore, a great temptation on the part of any losing party to try for a second "free bite at the apple," hoping that the Board will reverse the case in whole or in part; and, there is more than a minimal chance that some modification of the judge's decision will occur in the course of Board review.

---

[7] 41 NLRB ANN. REP. 209 (1976).

[8] 40 NLRB ANN. REP. 209 (1975) ; 35 NLRB ANN. REP. 158 (1970).

[9] 30 NLRB ANN. REP. 181 (1965).

[10] 15 NLRB ANN. REP. 230 (1950).

In 1974, a full sustaining of the judges' decisions occurred in 43.9 percent of the cases appealed to the Board. (This compares with 45 percent in 1973 and 61 percent in 1972.) On the other hand, complete reversal of the administrative law judges' decisions occurred in 1974 in only 6.8 percent of the cases (7 percent in 1973, 8 percent in 1972). But in 66.1 percent of the 1974 cases, there were some modifications made by the Board in the decision of the judge. These ranged from minor to major, an internal Board survey characterizing 17.6 percent as "minor," 21.4 percent as "partial," and 16.4 percent as "more grevious reversal." [11]

Since the NLRB currently reviews about 1,000 judges' decisions a year, exercises its discretionary review functions with respect to another 1,000 election cases,[12] decides a substantial number of interlocutory matters, and carries a variety of duties dealing with the general administration of the agency, it is only too obvious that five persons cannot, unaided, perform all of these tasks.

The Board is aided in its work by the Executive Secretary's office, which performs all of the duties normally performed by a clerk's office in an appellate court and provides many services which are now being performed by various types of court executives within the state and federal judiciaries. The Executive Secretary's office also assists the Board members and the Board chairman in various administrative tasks, particularly in maintaining communication between the Board and the regional offices in election case matters, in which the region's reporting responsibility is, in theory at least, to the Board.

The Executive Secretary's office is not only the principal communications link between the Board and the regions, but also is the principal communications link between the Board and the general public. While the Board's Division of Information provides the public with written materials and with news about the Board's operations, appointments, and a variety of other matters, the Executive Secretary's office tends to be the focal point for inquiries concerning the status of litigation pending at various levels within the agency. Frequently that office also serves as a buffer between the Board and members of the

---

[11] Data supplied by the Office of the Executive Secretary, NLRB.

[12] Data supplied by Office of Representation Appeals, NLRB. (In fiscal 1975, 1,047 Requests for Review were received, which was up from 756 in 1965.)

administration or Congress who may desire to communicate with Board members. Board members have for years refused to communicate with anyone about matters pending before the Board. This is sound judicial practice. But if a Congressman is asked by his constituent when he may get a decision in his case, the Congressman wants to communicate with someone. His inquiries, whether by telephone or letter, are consistently referred to the Executive Secretary for handling, thus insulating the Board members from any written or verbal communication in which the merits of the case might be touched upon.

The Board is also aided by attorneys who are assistants to individual Board members. Formerly called legal assistants, they have recently been retitled "counsels," with various levels of responsibility being recognized by title modifications, such as senior counsel, deputy chief counsel, and chief counsel. Each Board member has about twenty attorneys assigned to him for assistance in handling his quasi-judicial review function. How efficiently and promptly these staffs work will be examined in a later chapter. Here we wish to give only some indication of the nature and scope of the quasi-judicial review function which is performed in Washington, D.C., at the Board's headquarters by the Board members, their respective staffs, and subsidiary divisions such as the Executive Secretary's office, the Division of Information, and the Solicitor's office.[13]

Indeed, probably the most important and time-consuming of the duties of the members of the National Labor Relations Board is this judicial appellate review function which requires that the records of the trials conducted by the administrative law judges be reviewed, that possible errors committed by the judges be identified and duly considered, and that a review decision be written in each case. The business of judging the judges has become, after forty years, big business!

---

[13] The Solicitor was originally intended to be an advisor to the Board on miscellaneous legal matters arising principally out of administrative functions. The Solicitor currently, however, also performs work directly related to the Board's review function, such as assisting in drafts of summary judgment cases and assisting in presenting on short notice and with a minimum of study a review of the salient facts of interlocutory matters on which immediate Board decisions are necessary so that the progress of a trial will not be unduly interrupted. There is a staff of about five attorneys now assigned to the Solicitor's office.

DRAGGING THE RECALCITRANTS TO LAW

We have alluded to the lack of authority in the decisions of the Board's administrative law judges and in the decisions of the Board itself. We have mentioned that about 75 percent of all respondents take the free ride and appeal adverse decisions of administrative law judges to the Board. After the Board has reviewed the decisions, about 68.6 percent currently comply, but 31.4 percent go along for the ride to the next step—the court of appeals (see Appendix, Table 1; for all tables, see Appendix).[14]

A respondent can either sit and wait for the Board to go into court and enforce its order; or, taking the initiative in the court review process, a respondent may itself petition for review of a Board decision. In either event, the case ends up in the court of appeals, and somebody must brief it and argue it on behalf of the agency. This has always been regarded as a function of the five-member Board; but for many years, the Board has delegated that function to the General Counsel, who in turn has created a special Division of Enforcement Litigation. The bulk of the work of this division lies in attempting to secure enforcement of Board orders in the courts of appeals. In addition, there are a few cases which go to the Supreme Court which are handled by a special subdivision of this division. There is also some contempt litigation in the courts when a recalcitrant respondent will not comply even with a court of appeals order; and there is some miscellaneous, special litigation, such as some injunctive litigation (although most of this is now handled by regions), Freedom of Information Act cases, and a few other special kinds of court work, which is also handled by this division.

The number of cases taken to the courts each year has now reached the level of 250 or more cases annually.[15] In each of these cases, at least one brief and very possibly a reply brief must be prepared; and in many, oral argument will be required, although an increasing number of United States courts of ap-

---

[14] Note that the percentage of compliance without resort to litigation has climbed to this 68.6 percent figure in 1975 from only 42.1 percent a decade earlier.

[15] *See, e.g.*, 40 NLRB ANN. REP. 250 (1975); 41 NLRB ANN. REP. 254 (1976).

peals are now scheduling oral arguments in only a selected number of cases.

Thus, we see that the Board's role as public law enforcer is clearly manifold in function, administratively time-consuming, and substantial; but in the Board's history, its other role as honest ballot association has been equally, if not more, demanding. In 1977, the Board celebrated the fact that its thirty millionth employee voter had cast his ballot. How well has the Board administered this election-managing function?

CHAPTER IV

Thirty Million Voters and How They Grew

The store was not open long before the crowds came. In 1938, the third year of the Board's history, over 340,000 ballots were cast in Board-conducted elections. In that year, over 3,600 "R" cases (petitions seeking to have the Board hold an election) were filed, resulting in a total of 1,152 elections being conducted (Table 3). By 1940, the number of ballots cast had risen to over one-half million, and by 1942, it exceeded one million (Table 2). Those were the big years. Over one million voters cast valid ballots again in 1943 and in 1944—more than twice as many as would vote three decades later despite the vast increases in the nation's population and the size of its work force over those thirty years.

Election cases grew to be, by far, the biggest part of the Board's work, particularly at the midpoint of its first decade of existence. While charges of unfair labor practices exceeded election cases by a four to one ratio in the Board's first year (1936), the proportion had very nearly reversed itself by 1944, when over 6,600 election cases were filed, and less than 2,600 unfair labor practice charges were lodged with the NLRB.[1] According to the Board's 1942 *Annual Report*, election cases had already increased from 19 percent of its total workload in 1936 to 55 percent by 1942.[2] Yet resistance to the conduct of elections also apparently increased during this period. While in 1936 over 88 percent of its election cases were handled without the necessity of a hearing, that figure had dropped to 65.4 percent by 1945.[3]

By 1946, the number of petitions for elections had risen to over 8,000, and the number of elections conducted reached a

---

[1] 11 NLRB ANN. REP. 75 (1946).

[2] 7 NLRB ANN. REP. 2, 3 (1942).

[3] 10 NLRB ANN. REP. 12, 14 (1945).

new peak of over 5,500 (Table 3). The number of voters, however, had declined from the 1942-44 rate of over 1 million per year to approximately 700,000 in 1946 (Table 2). Whatever sighs of relief may have been breathed by ballot counters at the Board's regional offices as they watched this trend developing were short lived, for the trend was soon to be reversed by an act of Congress. In 1947, as part of the Taft-Hartley amendments, the Congress required that unions obtain authorization from employees by means of an election before they were entitled to enter into union security contracts which require membership in the union as a condition of employment. No such statutory requirement had existed prior to that time, and there were thousands of union security agreements which were put in jeopardy by the new legislation. The new law thus led to a rash of new elections, participated in by enormous numbers of voters, and the total votes soared to near the 2 million mark in 1948. In that year, of the nearly 2 million valid ballots, over 1,600,000 were cast in this new type of union shop authorization election, with the rest of the votes being cast in the standard representation case election wherein the employees were deciding which union, if any, they desired to represent them.

The boom began in 1948 and reached its peak in 1949, when a total of over 2 million valid ballots were counted (Table 2). Although the authorization elections required supervision and entailed plenty of chores for Board agents, they involved relatively little in the way of hearings or other contested matters. The Board's 1950 *Annual Report* states that less than 0.2 of 1 percent of these "UA" cases required a hearing, decision, or other formal action.[4]

As employees consistently voted by nearly unanimous votes in favor of union shop authorizations, the Congress was persuaded by 1951 that no truly useful purpose was being served by its 1947 "authorization election" requirements. Thus, on October 22, 1951, Congress repealed the statutory requirement for union shop authorization elections, substituting instead, however, a procedure by which employees could initiate a deauthorization petition to determine whether they wanted to *revoke* the authority of their bargaining representative to enter into union security contracts.[5] The number of voters in those de-

---

[4] 15 NLRB ANN. REP. 1 (1950).

[5] Pub. L. No. 189, ch. 534, 82d Cong., 1st Sess.

authorization elections has never achieved truly significant numbers and has not added substantially to the Board's election workload.

As is evident from Table 3, once the union shop authorization provisions were repealed, the Board's election case load flagged somewhat, dropping to a low of 7,165 petitions and 4,392 elections conducted in 1955—well below the over 10,000 petitions and nearly 7,000 elections of 1947. The number of voters in 1955 was even dramatically lower, falling to well under 500,000 from over 1 million in the early 1940s and from over 800,000 in 1947 (Table 2).

We are aware of no particular reason why 1955 marked such a low point in petition and election activity nor, for that matter, why 1959 again showed a sharp rise in election petitions filed. As pointed out in the Board's 1959 *Annual Report,* the Board conducted more elections in 1959 than it had since 1954 (actually, since 1953, as Table 3 indicates).[6] But Table 2 also shows that fewer employees voted in the 1959 elections than had voted almost two decades ago in 1940—and less than in any year in the late 1940s and the 1950s, except for 1958. One of the factors involved, as noted in the 1959 *NLRB Annual Report,* was that for the second time in five years more than 50 percent of the elections conducted by the Board involved less than thirty employees.[7] That was a harbinger of things to come.

By 1975, the average number of employees per election had declined to 48; and three-quarters of the elections conducted by the Board in 1975 were in units of 59 or less voters.[8] That average of 48 employees per election contrasts sharply with an average of over 280 voters per election back in 1941![9]

By the late 1960s and on into the 1970s, the general trend was toward a gradually increasing number of elections (with only an occasional year showing a modest decrease) but toward ever smaller voting units. The reports also show a trend toward an ever-decreasing percentage of union victories over the years, which may or may not be related to the voting unit size.

---

[6] 24 NLRB ANN. REP. 2, 3 (1959).

[7] *Id.* at 3.

[8] 40 NLRB ANN. REP. 16 (1975).

[9] Derived from 6 NLRB ANN. REP. 37 (1941).

Table 3 indicates that the agency, generally speaking, has kept up with the changing election case workload. It fell behind in its earlier years, closing less "R" cases than were filed within each of the first three years of its history. But then the trend was reversed, and Table 3 discloses that normally the " 'R' Cases Closed" very nearly parallel the " 'R' Cases Filed," thus demonstrating that no growing backlog of election petitions was ever allowed to develop. Even the flood of "UA" elections did not succeed in drowning the Board. Although in 1948 there were 26,099 such cases filed and only 17,958 elections held, by the very next year the Board was cutting back on its backlog, conducting elections at a faster rate than that at which it was receiving new petitions. Its backlog of total cases, which had reached 12,642 in 1948, was cut back to 5,722 in 1949, a normal "pending" case load for that period.

THE BOARD'S ELECTION EFFICIENCY

With what dispatch has the Board handled its election workload over the years? Statistics are scarce for the first decade of the Board's existence. Very scattered data will be found in the early *Annual Reports*, and requests made to the Executive Secretary's office failed to produce any reliable data for these early years. In 1946, however, representation cases requiring a Board decision took a total of 151 days from petition to Board decision—69 days from the date of filing to close of hearing and 82 more days from the close of the hearing to the issuance of the decision.[10] By 1950, the decision time from close of hearing to the issuance of the decision had been reduced from 1946's 82 days to 55 days (Table 4). Substantial improvement was also made in the prehearing time. In 1951, that time lapse had been reduced from 1946's 69 days to 55 days (Table 4), while the time lapse from close of hearing to Board decision in 1951 was down to 53 days. The time lapse from the filing of the petition to the close of hearing was cut under Guy Farmer's chairmanship in 1953 to 19 days—a radical reduction from the 55 days which existed in 1951. In 1953, also, the time lapse for arriving at a decision after the hearing was reduced from 1951's 53 days to 45 days. While the 19-day petition-to-hearing achievement proved to be only a one-year

---

[10] 18 NLRB ANN. REP. 2 (1953).

phenomenon, the time lapse from filing of petition to close of hearing has been held since that time, with but few exceptions, in the low 20s. For any government agency consistently to hold hearings on matters within three to four weeks of initial filings is a commendable record!

The 45-day median decision-making time in 1953 also proved to be a record for one year only. But until 1961, that decision-making time was kept within 50 to 60 days (with one or two exceptions). Here, too, a record of making decisions in a median time of less than two months is not a bad one. In 1961, the Board acted to delegate most of its election case decision making to the regional directors. Their track record has been even better. As shown in Table 4, the median number of days of decision-making time for regional directors has never exceeded 25 days! Those cases, however, which, since the 1961 delegation, have had to go to the Board in Washington for decision have not fared so well. Table 4 shows that such cases have consistently taken over 100 days; and in at least one year, the time required exceeded 150 days. This is, in part, a reflection of the fact that only the more difficult cases are sent to the Board for decision; but it is also a reflection of the fact that the Board's decision-making process have grown clumsy.[11]

But at least for the less complex contested cases—those in which the regional director now normally makes the decision—Table 4 shows that, except in 1971, the total of the time lapse from the filing of the election petition to the issuance of a regional director's decision has stayed under fifty days.

One occasionally hears horror stories, generally from unions, urging that some better and faster method be discovered to speed up the NLRB's election process. Usually some individual case is mentioned which has languished somewhere in the Board's structure for a year or so. There are, of course, such cases. Some issues prove knotty. Some bureaucratic oversights occur, resulting in temporarily misplaced files or other such accidents which can delay the process. An individual Board member may either have difficulty with, or be indifferent to, some particular case so that it stays in a pile of inactive matter on a corner of his desk. Even a regional director, who is subject to closer supervision than Board members, may occasionally do the same.

---

[11] The problems of decision making at the Board level are discussed in chapter VII.

But when the median time for the filing of a petition to the issuance of a decision and the direction of an election in a contested proceeding consistently runs at less than two months, and when elections by agreement occur in over 75 percent of the cases [12] and are fully completed within less than sixty days of the filing of a petition, it is obvious that the continuing complaints about the Board's timetables in election cases refer only to the isolated case. There is always room for improvement, but the administrative record achieved by the agency in its representation proceedings—except perhaps some of those which go to the full Board in Washington for decision—is one for which no apologies are needed.

EFFICIENCY AND THE REGIONAL DIRECTORS

There is another myth which is in need of debunking. It is commonly said, particularly by those who advocate a delegation of the Board's decision-making power in unfair labor practice cases, that the delegation of this power to regional directors saved the Board and parties who appear before it from utter chaos because the Board was proving unable to cope with its case level. The statistics render this myth suspect.

The delegation of decisional power to regional directors was authorized by the 1959 amendments to the Act, but the delegation power was not exercised until 1961. The Board does not appear to have been either on the brink of collapse or bogged down by hopeless delays at this time. In 1960, as is evident from Table 3, there were 10,130 election cases filed. Although this represented an increase from the number of cases filed in the immediately preceding year and the years of the mid-1950s, it was not as many cases as had been filed back in 1952, when 10,447 "R" cases were filed. Similarly, in 1960, the Board conducted 6,633 elections, an increase over the years immediately preceding, but less than the 6,866 elections conducted in 1952. Nor were long delays occurring in the decision-making process. In 1960, the time lapse from filing of petition to close of hearing stood at twenty-four days, a considerable improvement over the fifty-five-day and forty-day figures which existed in 1951 and 1952 (Table 4). The time between close of hearing and Board decision stood at fifty-four days in 1960, a figure not out of line with the figures for such time lapse throughout the 1950s.

---

[12] 39 NLRB ANN. REP. 16 (1974).

Nor does it seem to have been true that representation cases were being processed in timely fashion only by neglecting the unfair labor practice case load. Table 4 shows that the time lapse from judge's decision to NLRB decision was 149 days in 1960, a considerably better record than the 234-day lapse which had existed just two years earlier, certainly not a trend showing any rapid deterioration of case-processing times from those which had prevailed earlier in the decade. Table 3 also shows that there was no rapid growth of backlog at this time. In fact, at the close of 1960, there were less cases pending before the agency than there had been at the close of 1959. In 1961, in the first year of the delegation of powers, there was an *increase* in the number of cases pending at the end of the year, although there had been a much more modest rise in total case intake than had occurred during the years 1957 through 1960!

Thus, while the delegation to regional directors of the authority to make decisions in representation cases has served the agency well as the years have gone by, it was not the dramatic rescue from chaos which it is sometimes painted to have been. It should be noted that there were 10,130 "R" cases filed in 1960, and in 1975, this had risen only to 13,083—an average increase of less than 2 percent per year. That increase could quite obviously have been handled within the existing machinery and without delegation.

It is clearly easier, however, for a single regional director to arrive at a decision in a representation case than it is for five or even three Board members to agree on a decision. Thus, so long as regional directors' decisions are acceptable to the public, it is certainly administratively more efficient to let one person make the decision. In addition, most of the administrative responsibilities of the regional offices have been delegated to the General Counsel, and the kind of supervision that can be exercised by one single executive over regional office staffs is more workable than supervision by a five-person Board already having trouble keeping up with its own appellate decisional case load.

The regional directors' decisions have turned out to be palatable to the public. There was concern by both labor and management representatives in 1961 that this might not be so; but regional directors appear to have been able to develop perhaps greater expertise in the kinds of issues presented in representation cases than the Washington staffs of the Board members had or reasonably could be expected to have had. In difficult unit cases, knowledge of the industry is vital; and regional directors and their staffs become more familiar with the types of industries located in their particular areas than Board staff members sitting in Washington are likely to be able to become on a nationwide basis. So, while the delegation of election case decision making to regional directors has not been the life-saving miracle it is sometimes claimed to have been, it has been an administrative success. One hears almost no serious suggestions that it be revoked, narrowed, or substantially modified.

In fact, the entire record of the Board in playing its role as an honest ballot association appears to have been handled in an administratively sound fashion. That is why one also hears no serious proposals to divest the Board of its authority to play this significant role or to transfer that role to another agency or group.

Sam Zagoria, a former Board member, had a journalistic and public relations background. It was he who originated the idea of the Board's Twenty-Five Millionth Voter Celebration (of which the recent Thirty Millionth Voter Celebration was a copy). It was a success, and it was bound to be, for Sam had picked the least controversial aspect of the Board's work—one in which its operations have been much more efficient and successful than one might expect from even a small bureaucracy.

As an honest ballot association, the NLRB has proved itself honorable, able, and administratively sound.

CHAPTER V

The Wheat, the Chaff, and the General Counsel's Threshing Machine

We have already discussed briefly the functions of the General Counsel in connection with the Board's function as a public law enforcer. Administratively, the biggest and most important task performed by the General Counsel and his far-flung staff of lawyers and investigators is to take the very heavy volume of charges—currently over 30,000 a year—and to process them in such a way as to sort out the wheat from the chaff. The tables in the Appendix would indicate that there is today a good deal less wheat in proportion to chaff than in the early days of the Act. Table 3 shows the number of unfair labor practice cases closed in each year and also shows the number of cases in which some remedy was required—*i.e.*, all those in which a notice posting was ordered or agreed to. Since it is the agency's policy not to settle a case without at least a notice posting, the number of cases in which notices were posted must necessarily reflect all the cases in which the General Counsel or the Board determined that some remedy was necessary.

In 1939, there were 4,230 "C" cases closed and 903 cases in which some kind of remedy was required (Table 3). That indicates about a 21 percent ratio of wheat to chaff. In 79 percent the matter was closed through dismissal or withdrawal and thus without any remedy. In 1945, the ratio of remedy to no-remedy cases was a little higher—about one in four or 25 percent; in 1950, it was down to 23 percent. But by the mid-1950s, the percentage of "wheat" was down to 13 percent (in 1955) and a little less than 16 percent (in 1956). In 1960, the "some remedy" cases had climbed briefly to 19 percent; but in the 1970s, the percentages of remedy cases stayed within the narrow, and lower, range of from approximately 13 percent to 15 percent (slightly less than 13 percent in 1976).

Since other data show that over 90 percent of the agency's total "C" cases are closed without the necessity of any formal hearing before an administrative law judge, solely through the efforts of the General Counsel and his staff, it is reasonable to conclude that most—indeed, over 90 percent—of the sorting of wheat from chaff is done by the General Counsel's side of the agency.[1] After the issuance of a complaint, the judicial process is invoked, and there is further sorting of wheat from chaff. Some of this is by decision by an administrative law judge and/or the Board, although the General Counsel's forces are also a part of this process, functioning in their capacity as Messrs. District Attorneys. The efficiency and the dispatch with which the threshing machine operates is thus attributable in substantial degree to the operator of the machine—the General Counsel.

THE COMPONENTS OF THE THRESHING MACHINE

The components of the machine which accomplishes the sorting out of cases demanding a remedy from those without merit are people components—various administrative groups within the General Counsel's staff. Those groups fall into four general categories, which I shall call (1) the Laborers in the Thirty-one Vineyards, (2) the Feather Merchants, (3) the People in the Puzzle Palaces, and (4) the Maintenance Gang.

The Regional Office Staff

The Laborers in the Thirty-one Vineyards are the General Counsel's staff in the thirty-one regional offices (and a few subdivisions thereof called resident offices or subregional offices). In recent years, there have been in the neighborhood of 1,500 such Laborers—roughly one-third attorneys, one-third field examiners, and one-third nonprofessional personnel (Tables 5 and 6).

Middle Management

The work of these field offices is supervised and coordinated by the Feather Merchants—an intermediate level of middle management types officially known as Associate General Counsels, Deputy Associate General Counsels, and so on. They are frequently referred to as Feather Merchants by regional personnel, although

---

[1] *See, e.g.*, 41 NLRB ANN. REP. 5 (1976), showing 94.9 percent of cases closed by dismissal, withdrawal, settlements, and adjustments.

primarily in behind-the-back references. The slightly derogatory term is, I suppose, a reflection of the typical field office resentment of Washington supervision—a type of resentment not confined to the NLRB or to government. (Most plant managers of outlying plants with whom I have had the privilege of working in private practice have developed similar derogatory terms for the brass at corporate headquarters and feel the same underlying resentment of centralized control and supervision.) Yet the need for supervision and for readily available lines of communication between Washington and the field is real, and this middle management group has become, as the agency has grown and the volume of work expanded, a necessary group of contributors to the efficiency of the General Counsel's operation.

The Office of Appeals and the Division of Advice

The People in the Puzzle Palaces is a frequently used colloquialism for two similar, yet different, segments of the General Counsel's staff—the Office of Appeals and the Division of Advice.

When a regional director is unsure whether a complaint should issue on a particular charge, he may get legal guidance from the Division of Advice. Very often what is involved is a ticklish question of statutory interpretation or doubts caused by lack of clarity in the precedents established by Board and court decisions.

The Office of Appeals was created by the General Counsel some years ago so that a charging party advised by a regional director that no complaint would issue on his charge would have some avenue of appeal. When a charge is dismissed, the charging party is always advised that he has the right to appeal the matter to the General Counsel's Office of Appeals in Washington. If such an appeal is successful, the General Counsel will direct the regional director to reverse his initial decision and issue the complaint. Such reversals do not occur in any substantial number of cases, but the opportunity for an appeal from the regional director's determination is doubtless sound administrative practice and has helped blunt some of the criticism of the power vested in the General Counsel.

Former Senator Sam Ervin has referred to the General Counsel of the Board as "the keeper of the keys to the temple of justice," pointing out that he has virtually unlimited discretion in determining when and when not to prosecute on the basis of a charge brought to him. Any district attorney, of course, holds a similar set of keys, if that is what they are. But some avenue of appeal certainly does ease the tension created when a charging party has been told that he has no case. True, he cannot appeal beyond the General Counsel, but he can at least get his second bite at the apple and is more likely to feel that he has been accorded due process.

Under General Counsel Peter Nash, opportunity was frequently given to make personal appearances and arguments before the General Counsel and/or members of his staff in Washington in support of such an appeal. His successor, John Irving, has continued to accord this privilege liberally. This again gives a feeling of openness and directness, and hence credibility, to the General Counsel's determinations. The General Counsel's threshing machine is thus a better and more acceptable machine by virtue of this component.

The term *Puzzle Palace* symbolizes, however, the feeling of many regional personnel that these headquarters reviews—both by the Division of Advice and the Office of Appeals—are ivory tower in nature, made by professionals too far removed from the people and real life situations faced daily by the regional offices. Furthermore, because General Counsels have consistently taken the position that they should test the proper interpretation of the law by issuing complaints in doubtful cases, complaints may be ordered to issue by the Office of Appeals or Division of Advice in situations where a settlement-conscious, practical-minded regional director might have preferred to concentrate the efforts of his region on dealing with less esoteric instances of alleged law violations.

There have also been times when both of these offices have tended to operate too slowly, perhaps because the issues required study, perhaps also because they are distant from the pressure of the parties and secure in their offices on Pennsylvania Avenue in Washington. In recent years, however, these offices have operated with a minimum of delay, and the earlier criticisms of tardiness are now largely without justification.[2]

As an administrative matter, it is not easy to find qualified personnel who are willing to work in these offices. While the work has some interesting legal facets, such as exploring the

---

[2] According to data furnished by the Office of the General Counsel, NLRB, the Division of Advice's median processing time was twenty-five days in 1974, twenty-three days in 1975. The Office of Appeals' median processing time was fourteen days in 1974, eighteen days in 1975.

"cutting edges" of the law, it is a monastic kind of existence with very little contact with the public or opportunity to meet anyone other than one's co-workers. Since labor law is essentially "people law," it tends to attract lawyers who are not content with this kind of monasticism, and an assignment to the Puzzle Palaces is therefore widely regarded as an undesirable one. On the other hand, there have been truly brilliant lawyers, such as the late Gerald Brissman (former Associate General Counsel in charge of the Division of Advice), who have served the General Counsel and the public with dedication and distinction in performing this significant subfuncton.

The Division of Administration

What I have called the Maintenance Gang is the Division of Administration—a group providing the many needed support services, such as printing, duplication, personnel administration, janitorial services, arranging leases with private buildings for some regional offices, negotiating for proper space in governmentally owned buildings, budget and accounting services, administrative data gathering (by computer and by hand), and dozens of others. Such logistical support is required so that the professional staffs of both the General Counsel and the Board will have the tools necessary to do their jobs. Most of the personnel of this division are located in the headquarters offices of the Board in the Capitol.

It is difficult to judge how well the Maintenance Gang does its job. Even in industry, in the private sector, it is no easy task to manage "indirect labor" efficiently, or even to judge with any precision whether or not it is being efficient. At the NLRB, the necessary services are provided, and it is rare that the agency stumbles or falls because some needed administrative support is not there. Most of the agency's managers, however, have an uneasy feeling that this support could be better, and that its administration is more costly and less efficient than it might be; but there are almost no standards available by which to judge this service support function.

Since the key people of the agency are interested primarily in legal administration and are concerned with running elections, enforcing and interpreting the law, they are not willing to become deeply involved in the mechanics of support services. More than once, competent NLRB managers have refused opportunities to assume significant responsibilities in the Division of Administration. That, they have said, is not their cup of tea.

Other government agencies doubtless face the same problems. Many like to cook, but few enjoy doing dishes. So the dishwashing crew is often left to operate with only occasional supervision and is subject to little in the way of reliable measurement of productivity.

HOW LONG THE ROAD TO THE COURTHOUSE STEPS?— OR, HOW FAST DOES THE THRESHING MACHINE THRESH?

One of the tests of whether a public prosecutor is effectively performing his job is whether he is able to deal promptly with the charges brought to him by citizens. Promptness clearly benefits the charging party. Justice delayed *is* justice denied. But promptness also frequently benefits the charged party, who should not have to be under a cloud of uncertainty and face possible litigation over a long period of time. If the accused is innocent, he has a right to be declared innocent at the earliest possible date. If the matter must be litigated, it is to the advantage of both parties to have an early hearing while documents and witnesses are still easily available and the memories of witnesses are fresh.

The Statistics on Timeliness

In the early days of the history of the Board, however, either there was not a great deal of attention paid to timeliness or whatever efforts were made to achieve it were not particularly successful. Thus, in 1942, the median time from the filing of a charge to the holding of a hearing was *200 days!* [3] Although, by 1946, this had been improved somewhat, a 146-day time lapse from charge to hearing was nothing to brag about.[4] Indeed, the Board did not brag about it. It published no figures on time lapse during those years, although data was apparently kept somewhere in the Board's files, as sporadic revelations made clear, such as the figures I quoted above.

Most of the currently, readily available statistics are set forth in Table 4. An examination of those figures shows that

---

[3] 18 NLRB ANN. REP. 4 (1953).

[4] *Id.*

the time lapse from filing of charge to the issuance of complaint tended to be in excess of 100 days, with some few exceptions, until 1960. It is interesting to observe that, under the chairmanship of Guy Farmer, there was at least a short-lived interest in the need for expedition. One finds in the 1953 *Annual Report* a serious discussion of delay and the need for improvement.[5] An examination of Table 4 shows that this concern resulted in improvement, at least briefly. The investigatory time prior to issuance of complaint was cut from 160 days in 1952 to 129 days in 1953 and to *65 days* in 1954! But then there was silence in the *Annual Reports* again, and deterioration. Table 4 indicates that the successes of 1953 and 1954 were short lived, and the investigatory time lapse soon increased again to over 100 days.

With the advent of General Counsel Rothman in 1959, the trend was reversed, this time on a more lasting basis. Mr. Rothman insisted upon establishing and enforcing time targets for each phase of the threshing operation. This, we are told by veterans of the Board, did not endear him to his staff; but those were the days before militant public employee unions were around to cry "Speed-up!"[6] The adoption of these time targets (the current ones being pictorially represented in the illustration on p. 41) and the General Counsel's insistence that serious efforts be exerted to achieve them had a remarkable effect. Table 4 shows that the investigative time was sliced from 104 days in 1959 to exactly one-half of that figure—52 days— in 1960. It has hovered between 50 to 60 days ever since. Despite a tripling of the case load from 1960 to the present (" 'C' Cases Filed"—Table 3), the investigative time has remained well under control. As Table 4 indicates, that time crept up to near 60 days (and slightly over that in one year) in the late 1960s when Frank McCulloch was chairman and Arnold Ordman was General Counsel. Upon the advent of General Counsel Peter Nash in late 1971, however, that slippage stopped, and median times in the low 50s again became the norm.

---

[5] *Id.*

[6] When, as NLRB chairman, I attempted to improve the timeliness of processing of appellate decision making by the five-person Board, I was greeted with unfair labor practice charges filed by the Professional Association, a labor organization representing Board staff attorneys. A trial examiner of the Department of Labor found that the "unilateral" enforcement of time targets violated the Executive Order granting collective bargaining rights to public employee unions.

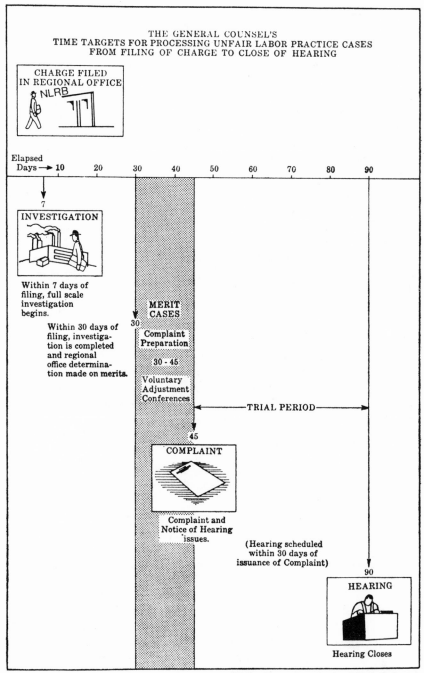

THE GENERAL COUNSEL'S
TIME TARGETS FOR PROCESSING UNFAIR LABOR PRACTICE CASES
FROM FILING OF CHARGE TO CLOSE OF HEARING

CHARGE FILED
IN REGIONAL OFFICE
NLRB

Elapsed
Days → 10   20   30   40   50   60   70   80   90

7
INVESTIGATION

Within 7 days of
filing, full scale
investigation
begins.

Within 30 days of
filing, investiga-
tion is completed
and regional
office determina-
tion made on merits.

MERIT
CASES

30

Complaint
Preparation

30 - 45

Voluntary
Adjustment
Conferences

←————— TRIAL PERIOD —————→

45
COMPLAINT

Complaint and
Notice of Hearing
issues.

(Hearing scheduled
within 30 days of
issuance of Complaint)

90
HEARING

Hearing Closes

National Labor Relations Board   Prepared by: Organization & Methods Branch
                                                      Division of Administration

The same table shows that this economy of time in the investigatory stages of unfair labor practice cases was not accomplished at the expense of letting representation cases lie fallow. The times from filing of petition to close of hearing in representation cases stayed only a bit over twenty days during the 1960s and 1970s, while at the same time the median time for investigating unfair labor practice charges stayed at about one-half the time used for this purpose during the 1950s and the even longer times which incomplete statistics indicate were apparently common in the 1940s.

The Laborers in the Thirty-one Vineyards may not have completely succeeded in meeting the targets set for them, but they have come close, as Table 4 will show. As depicted in the illustration on page 41, the time target for completing an investigation and issuing a complaint is forty-five days. This objective was achieved only in one year—1961. The current median times of just over fifty days may not hit the bull's-eye, but they are surely within the broad area of the target. The objective of completing the trial within another forty-five days has also not been fully achieved, but it, too, is not far out of reach of actual performance (*e.g.*, forty-eight days in 1974 and fifty-five days in 1975; Table 4).

How long, then, the road to the courthouse steps? On the average, the total median time from the day the charge is filed to the day the trial is over is pretty close to three months. We would venture to suggest there are very few agencies—federal or state—to which a citizen can go with a complaint and expect to have it investigated, a preliminary determination of merit made, and, if meritorious, a trial completed, all within three months of the date the citizen first walked into the agency's offices.

The road to the courthouse steps is not a long one.

The threshing machine threshes pretty fast.

THE GENERAL COUNSEL'S THRESHER AS A GROWTH INDUSTRY

Table 7 shows that the growth in the size of the bureaucracy at the NLRB has been substantial. Average employment has nearly tripled since 1940, and total compensation (over $47 million) is more than one hundred times larger than the $420,617 for 1935. Yet compared to growth figures for the federal bureaucracy as a whole, this is very moderate growth indeed.

The case load has increased sevenfold since 1940 (6,177 in 1940, 44,923 in 1975; Table 3). The personnel needed to handle those cases in timely fashion has not increased proportionately, having only tripled during this same period. The threshing machine has grown, but its productivity appears to have increased.

The Statistics on Productivity and Growth

Table 8 compares, for each year since 1951, the number of professional employees in all of the Board's regional offices (as taken from Table 5) with the total number of cases closed in each year (as taken from Table 3). The fourth column of the chart shows the average number of cases closed per regional professional staff member (a figure arrived at by dividing the number of cases by the number of professional employees). Admittedly, this is a rather crude statistic, and Table 8 does not pretend to be a precise or scientific productivity measure. Yet, since regional staff professionals are the principal movers and shakers in bringing virtually every representation case and unfair labor practice case to a conclusion, comparing the number of professional employees in the regions with the number of closed cases does have some meaning and, looked at over a period of years, gives some indication of productivity trends.

Table 8 seems to show that the productivity in the regions declined in the 1950s, slipping from fifty-three and forty-nine cases per professional in the first year or two of the decade to about forty cases per professional in 1958 and 1959. It declined still further during the 1960s, reaching a low of thirty-three cases near the middle of the decade. But during the 1970s, productivity appears to have improved by about 20 percent to over forty cases per professional. That is not only higher than the average for the 1960s, but is also higher than the average for the 1950s.

We have little data from the period before that. The 1961 *Annual Report* indicates that sixty-two professional employees were employed in the NLRB offices in 1936.[7] Since the records on cases closed show a total of 734 cases having been closed in that year,[8] it would appear that the average number of cases closed per regional professional in 1936 was 12—less than one-

---

[7] 26 NLRB ANN. REP. 1 (1961).

[8] 11 NLRB ANN. REP. 75 (1946).

third of the number in later years. Even making allowances for the fact that all of the procedures under the Act and the law itself were new at that time, it would seem that regional staff productivity in the early years must have been at an alarmingly low level. Or to put the matter more positively, just as timeliness has enjoyed a substantial improvement since the early days of the Act, so too has the productivity of the General Counsel's professional staff.

Empire Building and Costs

Tables 5 and 6 provide more detailed information about the composition of the staffs in various segments of the agency. They tend to show that bureaucratic empire building has, by and large, been avoided by this agency.

There is a tendency in many governmental agencies for Washington staffs to expand out of proportion to the growth in the field staffs who actually serve the public. No such disproportionate growth has occurred in the headquarters staff of the General Counsel. While professional field staffs grew from a total of 424 in 1951 to 984 in 1975, a 132 percent increase, the professional staff at the General Counsel's headquarters increased during that same time from 39 to 50, an increase of about 28 percent only (Table 5). The nonprofessional field staff expanded from 428 in 1951 to 588 in 1975, an increase of 37 percent, while the General Counsel's nonprofessional staff increased from 25 to 34 during the same period, an increase of an approximately 36 percent (Table 6).

Another bureaucratic tendency is for professional employees to build empires of nonprofessionals to serve them. This, too, apparently has been avoided by the General Counsel. In 1951, there was an almost 1:1 ratio in the field offices, which had a total professional employment of 424 and total nonprofessional of 428. In 1975, there were proportionately *less* nonprofessionals! As the regional offices expanded their professional employment to 984, nonprofessional employment increased only to 588.

Another area often worthy of scrutiny is whether the administrative support function has been allowed to grow out of control in terms of its ratio of personnel complement to the employees engaged directly in carrying out the mission of the agency. In 1951, the NLRB's Division of Administration comprised 27 percent of the Board's nonprofessional staff and 14 percent of its total staff. In 1975, those ratios were down, with administrative employees comprising 24 percent of the nonprofessional staff and less than 11 percent of the Board's total employment. The General Counsel has not, then, permitted the number of "overhead" or "indirect labor" employees to expand out of proportion to "direct labor."

The cost to the taxpayer, over the years, however, tends to dampen one's otherwise cheery spirits. As indicated in Table 7, while agency employment slightly less than trebled from 1940 to 1975, total compensation went up over twentyfold—from just under $2,266,000 in 1940 to over $47,800,000 in 1975. For this, however, we cannot hold either the General Counsel or the agency responsible. This represents the rise in the general level of government salaries and the toll taken by inflation. Like many other machines, although the General Counsel's threshing machine appears to have been improved and to have become more efficient in recent years, the doggone thing has sure gotten expensive!

CHAPTER VI

Don't Administer Me—I'm a Judge!

When the General Counsel has sorted out what he thinks is the wheat from the chaff, he then gets an opportunity to see whether one of the Board's administrative law judges will agree that it really is wheat.

This is the first judicial step in the public law enforcer process. It is also the first step in the processing of a case at this agency which comes under the supervision of the five-person Board rather than that of the General Counsel. At this point, we get our first look at how the five-person Board performs in administering those subfunctions of the public law enforcer process which come under its administrative supervision.

TIMELINESS AND PRODUCTIVITY

Table 9 is a statistical summary of the timeliness and productivity of the administrative law judges. We are once again handicapped by the lack of available data for the years preceding 1951. Only a smattering of information for those years can be gleaned from the *Annual Reports*, and the Board does not have readily available any information from its files prior to 1951.

The 1943 *Annual Report* tell us that administrative law judges (then called trial examiners) were getting their decisions out in about nine weeks (63 days) in 1942, and that this had been improved to five weeks (35 days) in 1943.[1] From the 1953 *Annual Report*, we learn that trial examiners were getting their reports out in an average of seven weeks (48 days) in 1946.[2] If this information is accurate, the Board's first-line decision makers were doing much better in the first decade or so of the

---

[1] 8 NLRB ANN. REP. 13 (1943).

[2] 18 NLRB ANN. REP. 4 (1953).

Board's existence than they have ever done since 1950. As Table 9 indicates, the time lapse from close of hearing to the issuance of decision had reached a median time of ten weeks (71 days) in 1951 and, by 1961, had stretched out to over fourteen weeks (99 days). Then, by about the midpoint of Chairman McCulloch's tenure, this delay increased to a new height of seventeen and one-half weeks (123 days) in 1965. After that, the record again improved considerably. The 1970s began with a median decision-writing time of 84 days; but as that decade rolled on, a more than 20 percent reduction to 69 days had been achieved by 1974. Table 4 indicates, however, that this progress was lost in 1975 and 1976, when the time lapse again climbed to 72 and 89 days, respectively.

Let us look now at productivity. During the 1950s, the productivity of the judges swung wildly between a high of fifteen cases per judge in 1951 to an unbelievable low of seven per judge in 1956 (Table 9). While improving to a level of nineteen cases decided per judge by 1960, the record slowly deteriorated in the following ten years, reaching a nadir of thirteen in 1970. Steady, but not dramatic, improvement was achieved in the first half of the 1970s at the rate of about one additional decision per judge per year, productivity reaching a maximum of seventeen decisions in 1974, but falling off slightly to sixteen in 1975.

So, on the average, the Board judges currently take a little over two months to write a decision after hearing the case and turn out (again on the average) a written decision about every three weeks. That is something less than a breathtaking pace.

These medians, although useful in analyzing the overall performance of the division, are doubtlessly unfair to a number of individual judges. There is a wide variation of both productivity and timeliness within the division, with some judges turning out more than double the median number of decisions in a median time of less than half the delay for the division as a whole. On the other hand, it is only fair to point out that there are also some judges with records of both productivity and timeliness which are far worse than the medians.

While there are no comparative measuring sticks readily available, almost any experienced labor practitioner viewing these statistics would, I am confident, conclude that both the work pace and the timeliness of the Board's judges are in serious need of improvement.

The Judge's Life

The judges themselves would take sharp issue with this—at least publicly and officially. Although the judges do not have a union as such, as have virtually all other NLRB employees, they have a *de facto* union which is effective both within and without the agency. There is an elected Committee of the Judges which meets with the administrative staff of the Division of Judges, and with the Board if necessary, to air judges' complaints. This is a powerful committee, which, by and large, has succeeded in blocking any significant disciplinary or control actions to improve the performance of the judges.

The judges also are quite influential beyond the bounds of the NLRB itself. They were very active and eventually effective in securing the title change from "Trial Examiner" to "Judge." They maintain good relationships with a number of senators and representatives on the Hill. There are both official and unofficial relationships between the Board's judges and administrative law judges in other agencies. Their joint efforts seem bent on preserving the *status quo* insofar as work demands are concerned, but they lobby incessantly for greater technical and clerical assistance, better salaries, and better "working conditions"—such as hearing rooms which, according to the judges, ought to look more like court rooms and to provide such luxuries as "chambers" for the judges and other accoutrements enjoyed by members of the federal bench.

In defending their record, the judges would point out that their work is not limited to the issuance of written decisions. They also are required to travel to places at which hearings have been scheduled, sometimes only to find that the matter had been settled without any notice to the Division of Judges. This happens only rarely, but the instances seem to remain firmly implanted in the judges' collective memory. They would also point out that they do achieve settlements in a number of cases, and that these are not reflected in the written decisions issued. This is true, although the Bar is well aware of the fact that only a few of the judges really make serious efforts toward settlement. Indeed, the Bar sometimes questions how far a judge can become involved in settlement talk without impairing his ability to hear and judge fairly the evidence when it is formally presented. Extensive involvement may mean that the judge may be prejudiced to some degree by the nature of the settlement discussions and the freewheeling discussion of the issues and the evidence which is essential to most successful settlement efforts.

I do not have available any hard data on the time which the judges may be required to spend in travel, settlement efforts, and other matters in addition to the hearing and deciding of cases. But, for whatever it may be worth, I offer my opinion, based on my experience as chairman of the NLRB and on my observations of over a quarter of a century of practice in the labor law field, that the time spent outside hearing and deciding cases is not enough to explain away the overall low rate of productivity of the division.

I recall a social function which I attended with one of the Board's judges. After a few cocktails, the judge grew expansive about the splendid life of an administrative law judge. He expounded upon the benefits of the semicontemplative long life, its leisurely pace, and its opportunities for not too rigorous travel around the country, and finally recommended to me that the Board ought seriously to consider utilizing the Division of Judges as a preretirement assignment for its loyal professional employees. It was, he said, not quite retirement but certainly far less rigorous than the demands on even the average field attorney. Similar admissions, not quite as dramatic as that one, have been made to me by other judges when talking with me privately and off the record.

When one considers that the average hearing before one of the Board's judges runs less than three days in duration and that the issues in the average case are fairly run-of-the-mill, it is difficult to defend a work pace which requires a decision to be written only about every three weeks and a median decision time of over two months.

Administrative Law Judges vs. *Federal and Other Agency Judiciaries*

Admittedly, however, we are without available standards for comparison. Federal court judges hand down a great many more decisions per year, but a number of their decisions are rulings from the bench not requiring any written opinion. Even when a federal judge's decision is reduced to writing, it sometimes consists merely of formal findings of fact and conclusions of law which can be compiled relatively quickly from the suggested findings and conclusions submitted by the attorneys for the parties. This is a procedure not used by the Board's administrative law judges nor, so far as I am aware, by administrative law judges in other agencies, and there is some question about whether it may properly be used under the governing Administrative Procedures Act.

Some comparisons have been attempted with judges from other agencies, but the results are inconclusive because the work of federal administrative agencies is so varied in character. An administrative law judge of the Federal Trade Commission, for example, will, with considerable frequency, have very long cases with a multitude of documents—a situation quite unlike the Board's rather steady volume of relatively short hearings. The judges hearing Social Security cases turn out a good many more decisions than the Board's judges turn out, but the typical Social Security hearing involves simpler and fewer issues and, often, fewer credibility questions than a typical NLRB hearing involves.

What are the causes and possible cures for a record on the part of the Board's judges which is in such obvious need of improvement?

HOW THE CIVIL SERVICE COMMISSION KEEPS IT ALL IN THE FAMILY

Lying at the root of the administrative problems of the Board's Division of Judges is the incredibly bad application and selection procedure which hog-ties the Board in its hiring of judges.

In 1972, the Board issued a press release announcing that it was "urgently" seeking well-qualified applicants for the position of administrative law judge. The news release was incorporated by the Associated Press in a story which appeared in over 100 newspapers across the country, including many major metropolitan dailies. That news release, plus some personal efforts on the part of the Board members to interest qualified practitioners in applying, resulted in our receiving approximately seventy-five letters from interested persons. We sent all seventy-five an explanation of the application process and a personal letter of encouragement from me. Only twelve actually applied!

Puzzled by this lack of follow-through, I wrote to all of the persons who had initially responded, inquiring about their loss of interest. Some twenty offered reasons which were either personal or which evidenced obvious deficiencies in background or experience. But the remaining responses—and we heard from most of the people to whom we wrote—showed that there were very serious problems with the recruitment and selection processes of the Civil Service Commission. The cumbersome, red-tape-filled application process succeeds in discouraging most applicants.

Here are some typical comments taken from the letters which we received. The following quotation is from an attorney with over eleven years of relevant experience, both in the labor relations field and as a trial lawyer, including two years of experience as an attorney with the National Labor Relations Board:

> My reason for not responding was primarily based upon the fact that the requirements of the application—i.e. lengthy data to be supplied, oral and written tests, and travel for interview, coupled with the time factor involved before an appointment could be made, as well as the uncertainty thereof, led me to conclude that at least the Civil Service Commission was not interested in my application for any reason except to use it in a statistical way to show that they were really trying to fill those positions with applicants from outside the government. . . . Only a government employee could wait for the period of time necessary to complete the requirements of the appointment without doing a grave injustice to either his clients or his employer in the private sector. . . . Accordingly, I concluded that the effort involved far outweighed the opportunity to achieve the desired objective, and accordingly did not respond.

Here is another, from a judge in a state court:

> After some 19 years in the practice of law, including nine years of extremely active work in the field of labor-management disputes and acting as impartial arbitrator in approximately 20 years as acting judge of the Superior Court, and having heard approximately 200,-000 matters during this period of time, I was not about to undertake to fill out the unwieldy and complicated application furnished me.

An attorney who had spent four years with the Board in the active trial of labor relations cases, who had since been in private practice and had written extensively in the field in scholarly publications, put it more simply:

> Not only do I not have the time to spend to fill out the onerous and forbidding Civil Service application, but I also consider it an indignity.

Another poignant remark came from a man who was chief litigation counsel for a law firm in a large city and had con-

ducted substantial labor litigation in the federal courts and before the Board. He said he thought that becoming a judge
would be "the natural outgrowth of this experience" and that it
could be "professionally fulfilling"; but then he commented:

> It seems obvious that you as Chairman have properly concluded that
> the efficiency and value of an agency depends upon its ability to re-
> cruit the best possible personnel. You have made serious efforts
> to stimulate people to seek employment with your Agency. The
> letter and application forwarded to me by the Civil Service Com-
> mission effectively destroys any specific enthusiasm generated by
> your activity.

The other responses received were similar. They leave little
doubt but that Civil Service Commission procedures have effectively discouraged many good candidates from applying for the
Board's judgeship.

There was a second category of replies that also troubled
me. About 22 percent of those responding stated that they did
not follow through with an application to the Commission because
they failed to meet the present stated requirements; but in each
such case, the length and scope of relevant experience, if accurately described in their letters to me, seemed to demonstrate
at least *prima facie* qualification for consideration.

For example, one such man had been an attorney for twenty-two
years but could not demonstrate the required amount of recent
trial experience (two out of the last seven years). This was
because he had been in labor relations work for the last thirteen
years, conducting arbitrations, handling grievances, and handling
contract negotiations; but, as his responsibilities in labor relations increased, he assumed more and more of the role of coun-
selor and advisor and moved further away from trial-related
work.

Another attorney with an extensive practice admitted that he
could not document the required amount of active trial experience over the past seven years. Yet he was a past president of
an academy of trial attorneys in one of our large cities. As he
said:

> Even among the so-called "trial specialists" the number of cases
> actually tried is not great. Approximately 95 percent of all cases
> (other than divorce, collection or minor matters) are disposed of
> without a judicial determination. It's a good thing that this is so,
> for if more than 5 percent of the civil and criminal cases were to
> be tried, the Courts would grind to a halt.

He goes on to say, with a touch of cynical wit:

> Attorneys like Melvin Belli and F. Lee Bailey would have little difficulty in qualifying. But while nothing in life is absolutely certain, it is unlikely they will apply.

His conclusion is less flippant:

> By diminishing the stress on recent trial experience, the standards would in no way be lessened and could in one sense be enhanced, for a trial specialist is not likely to be of the best judicial caliber, whereas a broad general practice coupled with some trial experience would seem to be the best qualification, given judicial temperament, analytical and writing ability.

Still another attorney with very considerable experience could not meet the recent trial experience requirement and commented that "judges serving on our Supreme Court bench in this State could not meet your Civil Service requirements." He went on to say, "I am not surprised that few people applied. Yet I regret that I had to decline making application because I have been active in the labor relations practice for over 18 years."

Those were the comments of the practicing lawyers who decided rather quickly that they did not, after all, want to be judges. Were their comments fair?

The Civil Service Commission's Idea of Qualifications

The Civil Service Commission announcement which is sent out to persons indicating interest in becoming an administrative law judge reads, in part:

> every applicant must include in his application a list, in chronological order, of a sufficient number of administrative law cases in which he has participated or court cases which he has prepared and tried, or heard, to demonstrate 2 full years (400 workdays) within the 7-year period immediately preceding the date of his application. He must show for every case so listed:
>
> 1. Title and citation.
> 2. Dates between which participation took place.
> 3. Brief statement of issues involved.
> 4. Regulatory body or court hearing case.
>
>   Note: For each court so cited, indicate whether Federal, State, or local; extent of jurisdiction (limited or unlimited, original or appellate).
>
> 5. Number of workdays spent in handling case, and in what capacity, i.e., judge, attorney, etc.

6. Names and current address of

   (a) Hearing Officer of regulatory body or of judge who heard case

   (b) Co-counsel, if any

   (c) Opposing Counsel

   (d) Names of Counsel appearing in case, if applicant claims qualifying experience in a judicial type position.

The applicant is also required to submit the details listed below regarding two of the cases referred to above which, in his opinion, are the most important ones in which he has participated. (If the applicant satisfies the administrative law, actual trial, or judicial requirements of this announcement by listing only one case, he may submit details on only that case). If the applicant claims that his experience satisfies any of the special qualifications for filling specific Hearing Examiner positions which are described beginning on page 18, at least one of the cases must have been in the field of the legal specialty involved.

1. The precise nature and extent of participation.

2. Full statement of issues involved and a description of the problem.

3. Outline of arguments made.

4. Summary of technical, economic or other data presented, including sources, manner of analysis, and uses, written decisions or opinions, or other papers prepared by applicant in one case.

5. Briefs, Memoranda of Law.

To assist the rating panels in determining the ability of the applicant to write clearly, concisely, and convincingly, the applicant shall submit with each such written decision or opinion a verification in the form of a signed statement of the extent of his personal involvement in and his responsibility for the preparation of the document; and the names and current addresses of those persons, if any, who worked with him in the preparation of the document.[3]

There can be little doubt that the enormous chores required to comply with stipulations like the above discourage most lawyers—particularly successful lawyers—from applying for a judgeship. Nor is even that red tape the totality of the process. In addition to documenting all of the above information, the applicant must subject himself to a six-hour written examination and a full one-hour individual interview set at a time and place convenient for the Civil Service Commission, with travel thereto being at the applicant's expense. Meanwhile, the applicant must have given

---

[3] U.S. CIVIL SERVICE COMMISSION ANNOUNCEMENT No. 313, October 1973, at 11-12.

full information about his references, with the understanding that the Commission might check them even prior to determining that he is a reasonably well-qualified applicant. That means that a practicing lawyer would have to expose himself to inquiries of his partners and of his clients, even if the Commission was not going to consider him seriously. That alone succeeds in discouraging a number of applicants. And after all of that, the applicant succeeds only in getting his name on the "Civil Service Register," thus making him available for possible selection by the NLRB or some other agency; but there is no guarantee that, by the time the Commission has completed its cumbersome processes, there will be any vacancies left to be filled.

The qualifications set by the Commission are in many respects unrealistic. The requirement that, in each of two full years within the past seven, the applicant must have devoted a full 400 workdays to the preparation and trial of administrative law cases screens out most successful practitioners. As a lawyer becomes successful, he spends less, rather than more, time in the court room or hearing room and tends to spend an increasing amount of time counseling his clients, leaving much of the time-consuming trial preparation and litigation to experienced junior lawyers. Nor is any credit whatever given by the Commission for the teaching of law. Thus, if a lawyer practices from age twenty-six to thirty-five and then goes to teach law at a major university for the next six years, he becomes automatically ineligible for appointment to a judgeship.

As the above comments suggest, the Civil Service Commission procedures have a strong tendency to keep these judgeships "in the family." That is to say, it is most often the salaried government lawyer, not needing to bill his time to clients, who can find the time to go through the lengthy and burdensome Commission requirements for application, testing, and interviewing. And the fair-to-middling government trial lawyer is the one most likely to meet the ivory tower requirements established by the Civil Service Commission. Eager and ambitious, hardworking private practitioners of the type that is, with some regularity, selected for federal judgeships in the judiciary are likely to be effectively screened out by the bureaucratic application and selection procedures of the Commission.

The Commission, however, has consistently refused to recognize the effects of its ill-designed processes. Repeatedly, in conference with Commission officials, I met with total resistance to any suggestions that this process could be simplified or made more realistic. I was with some frequency told that a former chairman of the NLRB—Frank McCulloch—participated in designing the requirements and procedures, the suggestion being that a brash subsequent chairman had no right to advise that they were working badly. Written demands for change resulted in replies rich in bureaucratic prose, but devoid of any hint of possible movement. After I left the Board, my successor, Chairman Murphy, expressed great hope that she would succeed in making a dent in the Commission's tough exterior; but over two years elapsed, and there were no more signs of movement at her urging than there had been at mine. The American Bar Association has joined in the effort to try to move the Commission on this point, but thus far to no avail.

We have here a classic example of the nearly insoluble problems which sometimes lie in the way of improving governmental administration. An agency faced with a problem, finding that one of the solutions must lie in better recruitment procedures, is stymied by the unwillingness of another administrative agency to change its encrusted ways of doing things. When this occurs, the only solution is congressional action. But a Congress, dealing with a thousand matters of national importance, is simply not likely to take the necessary time to develop on its own a better selection and application system which would probably have application to only a few hundred governmental positions per year. This leaves the initial agency with no help from the sister agency and no real likelihood of getting the problem resolved through legislation. It is a real lesson in the evils of bureaucracy.

NO CARROT AND NO STICK

Not only are the selection processes unsatisfactory, but the administrative tools available to the agency in attempting to improve the performance of its administrative law judges are almost nonexistent. The usual tools of both the private and public sectors are, simplistically stated, the carrot and the stick. Efficient performance should be rewarded by promotion and/or raises; inefficient performance should predictably result in demotion, discipline, or, in extreme cases, discharge. The sad, practical fact is that none of these motivational tools are adequately, if at all, available to the Board in dealing with its administrative law judges.

The Board's Administrative Ability to Discipline

Demotion, discipline, and eventual discharge for inefficient performance are not available in a true sense anywhere in the government. The lengthy procedural and substantive protections afforded to our civil servants through Civil Service Commission procedures effectively discourage most government administrators from really trying to make demotions or disciplinary measures stick, except in the most extreme cases. Even then, the attempt is too often stymied; and in many instances, the employee is allowed to linger on at pay status in a state of suspended animation while all of the long "due process" procedures are being carried out. This sometimes presents a worse administrative problem than if no action at all were undertaken. In addition to the Civil Service protections, government employee unions have now negotiated still further forums for challenging any kind of adverse actions, such as the imposition of either discipline or demotion.

All of these discouragements, plus some more, inhibit any such actions against administrative law judges. The Administrative Procedures Act does vest a large measure of independence in the administrative judiciary, and the imposition of any form of discipline on administrative law judges is further discouraged by the provisions of this Act. We have already described the aura of independence surrounding the corps of judges employed by the Board and have alluded briefly to the committee which Board judges elect to protest any interference with that cherished "independence." The psychological impact of this obsession with independence cannot be overestimated.

The principal administrator of the Division of Judges is the chief administrative law judge. He is appointed from among the judges in the employ of the Board and gains in neither job rank nor pay by this service; thus at the very outset, a sense of identification with his fellows is created which can easily run deeper than any loyalty to the Board or to any ideas about improving efficiency. The concept of disciplining one of his colleagues and of facing accusations of interfering with their treasured independence is sufficient to intimidate many a chief administrative law judge.

I appointed a rather crusty gent to serve as chief administrative law judge, partly because I believed he would have sufficient "guts" to take whatever action might be necessary to improve the efficiency of the division. He was bitterly resented by many of the judges, and virtually every effort at improvement was resisted. Yet, he persisted in avowing that he would take disciplinary action in necessary cases. Despite carefully organized resistance to his demands, there was nevertheless steady improvement in both productivity and timeliness of decisions under his tenure. He has since resigned as chief judge.

The most gentle of disciplinary measures—such as a refusal to send a judge to hear a case in a preferred city, because he was behind schedule in getting out a previous decision—caused roars of protest from the Committee of Judges. The idea that an inefficient judge could have his tenure in office threatened caused anguished screams of protest even from the most able, hardworking, and distinguished of the judges' corps, who rose to their inefficient comrades' defense. The use of harsh words against a flagging judge was said by the committee to be an insult to the dignity and integrity of all the judges. The defense mechanism is an entrenched and powerful one.

The Lack of Rewards

Because there are severe limitations on the exercise of disciplinary authority throughout the government, the carrot is a more useful tool in the hands of a government administrator than the somewhat frail stick. It is possible within the governmental wage structure to encourage the good performer by salary increases earlier than usual, prompt promotion, and various kinds of monetary awards. Although ceilings on government pay are lower than those in the private sector, beneath that ceiling there is opportunity for economic motivation. Particularly during the early stages of a government employee's career, monetary incentives can fairly readily be provided and are frequently effective.

No such incentives whatever are available to encourage better performance by administrative law judges. All law judges are in the same pay grade and receive only time-in-grade increases. The Civil Service Commission will allow nothing else. There is no possibility of hiring judges at lower grades and promoting them if their performance is better than average. There is, furthermore, no possibility of demoting a judge to a lower labor grade.

In addition, once again the aura of independence discourages even nonmonetary rewards. In one year, I sent letters of commendation to judges who had turned in a higher than average number of decisions and achieved better than average promptness in their decision making. Although most private and public employees react positively to commendations or compliments on their performance, this was not the case in this instance. Instead, some of the recipients, as well as the Committee of Judges, protested the commendations on the remarkable theory that this somehow interfered with the individual judge's independence. I was dumbfounded! But since commendations apparently had a negative incentive value within this group, I saw little point in utilizing them in subsequent years.

The concept that administrative law judges are somehow superhuman and require neither carrot nor stick to improve their performance seems to be a well-accepted myth within the bureaucracy. It is of course absurd. The results summarized in Table 9 show its absurdity. Our court systems labored long under the impression that individual judges were to be left to their own discretion in handling their case load efficiently and with dispatch. The judiciary is in the course of abandoning that theory, and the advent of court executives and an increasing wielding of authority by a judicial hierarchy is becoming the order of the day. But the administrative judiciary which wants the full title, compensation, and accoutrements of the true judiciary is unwilling to budge from its anachronistic habits. It is encouraged in that refusal by the Civil Service Commission and by the perhaps unintended effect of the Administrative Procedures Act.

The structure and framework of the administrative judiciary will not permit the use of either carrot or stick to improve the performance of those persons who serve as administrative law judges. This renders almost futile any serious effort to improve the timeliness or the productivity of the Board's administrative law judges.

That is the discouraging truth.

WHAT OF THE FUTURE?

If the present is that discouraging, what of the future? What is the solution?

In this author's opinion, there can be no effective solution without major changes in the structure. It will take congressional action to effect any meaningful changes.

The Civil Service Commission may, in time and at its typical snail's pace, revise its application forms and perhaps pay lip service to improving some of its selection procedures. The typical response of a bureaucracy under pressure is to make some changes so as to enable it to profess having heeded valid criticism. But the true bureaucrat knows how to do that without substantially modifying the *status quo*. The Civil Service Commission is one of the nation's most expert bodies at doing just that, and my hunch is that that is what they will do—slowly—here.

If there is to continue to be an administrative judiciary (a premise with which the author has less than full sympathy), it can be soundly administered only if three very basic changes are made in the present system. The management of the agency must be given the following basic tools: (1) control over the hiring process, (2) available monetary incentives, and (3) a clear and unmistakable right to demote and remove unproductive judges.

Control of Hiring

In my view, the experiment of taking the hiring control in all major respects away from the agency by vesting recruiting and qualification determination largely in the Civil Service Commission has proved to be a serious and costly mistake. It is, in fact, amazing that the ability level of the administrative law judges employed by the Board and other agencies is as high as it is when one views the really awful application and selection procedures which have been in effect now for a good number of years. There is little reason why the agency should not be given full control over the hiring of its administrative law judges.

There are those who will remind us that selection through the Civil Service Commission was determined upon in order to prevent political favoritism from governing the appointment of decision makers. Experience suggests that this is not a significant worry in the case of appointments made by the NLRB.

The Board, aided by the recommendations of the General Counsel, has for years appointed the regional directors who make the significant first-line decisions in representation cases. There is less criticism among the Bar of those decisions—and implicitly of the decision makers—than of the decisions of some of the Board's administrative law judges. Yet the Board has virtually full control over the appointment of its regional directors. Still, the Civil Service Commission argues that it must retain effective control over the qualifications procedures for administrative law judges. Why?

In the labor relations field in which it operates, the Board has, no doubt, been kept healthy in many respects by the fact that parties of predictably conflicting interests regularly appear before it. Thus, powerful interest groups representing labor and powerful interest groups representing management are constantly on the alert for any signs of possible antilabor or antimanagement bias on the part of the Board's decision makers as well as for any possible hint of corruptibility which might aid the opposing interests. I have no doubt but that the fact that no real scandal has beset the Board in its over forty years of existence is due in substantial part to this continuing watchful surveillance by an ideologically divided constituency. These countervailing forces would be equally effective in monitoring the Board's choices of administrative law judges if those forces knew that it was really the Board which was making those choices.

Monitors under Board-controlled Hiring. If the Board were to appoint administrative judges to sit in particular areas (rather than, as at present, to dispatch all of its judges from two centralized headquarters—one in Washington and one in San Francisco), that bipartisan surveillance would be even more effective. A judge may now decide one case in one area of the country and not be sent back there again for a very long period. This has the effect of precluding the Bar in any locality from having a really extended or concentrated view of the performance of any individual judge.

If judges were appointed to serve in a particular geographic area, there would be better opportunity for the representatives of both unions and management to observe their conduct. Any bad appointments would be quickly caught and publicized. (A further healthy effect would be to create pressure by real people for prompt decisions—pressure from which the judges comfortably situated in Washington and San Francisco are all too well insulated today.)

Another factor suggests that Board selection of judges would be effectively monitored from yet another quarter. It has become the tradition that three members of the Board are to be members of the incumbent president's political party, while two are to be members of the opposite party. Since judicial selection would thus be made by a two-party Board and would be carefully watched by party loyalists of both major parties, the appointment of incompetent political hacks under a spoils system would be minimized.

My own experience also teaches that there is rarely serious disagreement among the Board members about the qualification of a judge under consideration. Although the Civil Service Commission must now handle all the initial selection qualifications, the ultimate selection of the judge even now rests with the Board. The Board is seriously interested in getting good judges partly because a good decision by a judge makes its own review decision much easier. Secondly, Board members do hear criticisms from the Bar of judges whose performance is less than judicial, and they know that criticism reflects upon the entire agency. As a private practitioner before coming to the agency, I would much prefer that the NLRB, an agency which has proven reasonably responsive to well-based criticism from the citizenry and especially from the industrial relations community, have primary responsibility for the appointment of administrative law judges, rather than the distant, unresponsive, bureaucratically encrusted Civil Service Commission.

The ABA and Rating the Judges. If the appointment of administrative law judges were restored in full to the Board, where it belongs, the Board would be well advised, however, to work out with the American Bar Association's Labor Relations Law Section a means of soliciting comments or ratings from the Bar for any intended appointments. The ABA Labor Law Section is comprised of lawyers who regularly represent unions, lawyers who regularly represent management, and lawyers who serve as neutrals, such as arbitrators. Its various standing committees have developed a very constructive relationship among these representatives of diverse interests, and they have learned to cooperate successfully in many areas. Experienced labor law practitioners on both sides of the bargaining table are sincerely interested in having competent judges who will be fair and judicious in their approach to cases. Experienced labor lawyers representing management and labor respectively would, I believe, have relatively little difficulty in reaching agreement on the competence of proposed new appointments to the Board's administrative law judge corps.

The ABA's Labor Law Section has learned, because of the sometimes diverse interests of its members, to operate by consensus rather than by any kind of majority or plurality vote. Thus, a screening committee established by the Bar would, doubtless, report back favorably on those candidates on whom a consensus of opinion could be reached affirming their competence. To the extent that there were serious differences of opinion among the members of such a screening committee, the committee could simply report this fact, which would be enough to indicate that there was concern in one segment or another about the judiciousness or competence of the proposed candidate. That information would be very useful to the Board in making its appointments. It might on occasion choose to disregard an indication of some dissatisfaction among the members of the Bar, particularly if its own research indicated the likelihood of a judgment error on the part of the Bar, but I would expect that the Board would heed, most times, the Bar's recommendations, which would provide an additional safety factor against the appointment of either biased or incompetent judges. In my opinion, that kind of screening would be far more effective and reliable than the complex screening today engaged in by the Civil Service Commission.

Monetary Incentives

In addition to control over the hiring process, the Board needs monetary incentives to motivate judges to utilize their best efforts to render prompt decisions and to budget their own time in a prudent manner so as to enable them to handle the maximum number of cases per year consistent with their respective physical and mental capacities. Provided with that significant motivational tool, the Board could then do with its judges much the same thing that former General Counsel Rothman and his successors did so successfully with field examiners and field attorneys —*i.e.*, establish time targets and demand that they be met.

I am not suggesting arbitrary and inflexible administration of such targets. Obviously a very long and complex case will take longer to decide than a simple one. The General Counsel and his regional directors have recognized that fact and do not expect their time targets to apply arbitrarily to every single case. The targets are norms and are used as norms in day-to-day administration.

Furthermore, the ability of able, experienced judges to handle complicated cases within, say, 120 days would have to be recognized as being as worthy of monetary reward as the ability of a bright, young new judge to turn out a decision in a simple case within 30 days. But a clear recognition that judges, like lawyers and investigators, are expected to meet certain standards of timeliness and certain standards of productivity is long overdue at the National Labor Relations Board. There is no realistic hope of succeeding in effectuating a recognition of such requirements by judges unless those judges who will meet such standards can be rewarded for so doing.

It should therefore be clear that within-grade increases, sustained superior performance awards, and other forms of monetary recognition utilized elsewhere in the career service need to be available to the Board's administrators in dealing with the Division of Judges. In addition, the Board should be able to employ new judges at one or two salary grades below the maximum grade available for experienced judges. This is not now possible, again because of a Civil Service Commission bureaucratic tenet that a judge is a judge is a judge. The prevailing myth is that, if an agency can promote a judge, it will use such promotions to shape the judge's decisions to policy lines that are approved by the agency. That, in my opinion, is nonsense and is no excuse for a failure to give candidates with perhaps eight or ten years of experience a reasonable beginning salary and an opportunity to advance to higher salaries on the basis of merit and experience. It is absurd to lump all the good, the bad, the experienced, and the inexperienced judges within the narrow confines of a single labor grade.

Strengthening the Board's Administrative Ability to Discipline

While in government service the carrot is much more effective than the rather wobbly stick available through discipline and discharge, Congress should at least make it plain that judges who fail consistently to achieve reasonable standards in promptness and productivity can be demoted and removed. I recognize full well that Civil Service traditions are such that any such right will be encumbered by the elaborate set of protective devices generally available to career government employees. I also recognize that there is today, in theory, a right vested in the Board to remove incompetent judges, a right subject to the right of the judge to a hearing and the usual protections. Yet, because the route of demotion and removal ought to be plainly available and since there is developing a very real belief on the part of many that any attempt to remove a judge because of inefficiency must be construed as an interference with his judicial independence, Congress should provide a much needed clarification. It should say, simply and directly, that the right to demote and remove for inefficiency or incompetence does exist. Such a statement of congressional intent would clear the air which has been cloudy for too long a time.

CONCLUSIONS

To achieve this restoration of hiring control to the Board, to make available to the Board monetary incentives, and to reestablish a clear and unmistakable right to demote and remove unproductive judges will take congressional action. From information received from friends and acquaintances who served as chairmen or members of other governmental agencies which employ administrative law judges, I sense that the NLRB's problem of being unable to administer its Division of Judges effectively is not peculiar to the Board. It cannot be in the best interests of the government and of the public to permit administrative law judges in any agency to continue to enjoy an exemption from effective administration. Congress ought, therefore, to look carefully at the outmoded and cumbersome selection procedures and the lack of motivational tools which seem to plague all federal agencies and to deter them from achieving workable administration of administrative law judges. It may be that different solutions are required in different agencies. But anyone who knows the facts knows that the problem is basic and severe, and that new solutions are badly needed.

We can no longer afford to let administrative law judges tell their agencies and their real bosses—the taxpayers—"Don't administer me! I'm a judge!"

CHAPTER VII

Assembly Line Appellate Review— Does It Work?

The five presidentially appointed Board members constitute the small end of an increasingly large filtering funnel. Much is filtered out before it reaches that small end, but what is left is enough to threaten to jam the small end. In fiscal year 1974, the regional offices filtered out some 20,000 charges—25.5 percent by adjustment before an administrative law judge's issued decision, 36 percent by withdrawal, and 32 percent by administration.[1] Only 1,715 were actually tried before the administrative law judges (Table 10), and further filtering meant that the judges issued written decisions in 1,519. Still more were settled or the decisions complied with, and the Board in that year decided 1,195 cases (Table 10) in a total of 977 written opinions (Table 12).

The filtering funnel is large. It is comprised of some 1,400 field personnel at the top of the funnel (Tables 5 and 6), 80 to 100 administrative law judges in the midsection of the funnel (Table 9), but at the narrow end of the funnel are just five Board members.

In that same year (1974), there were also poured into the top of the funnel some 14,000 election cases (Table 3). About 83 percent were filtered out in the regions by being resolved without the necessity of a hearing and thus without the need for judicial decision.[2] Regional directors were also able to resolve posthearing matters in most cases. But the Board was confronted in that year with 665 requests for review of regional directors' decisions. There were also 142 requests for review of regional directors' supplemental decisions, and 119 requests for

---

[1] 39 NLRB ANN. REP. 11 (1974).

[2] *Id.* at 214.

review of regional directors' administrative dismissals, making the total requests for review in that year number 926.[3] Thus, at the narrow end of the funnel, the five members of the Board had to deal with 926 requests for review and 156 contested election case decisions (Table 12), and had to issue nearly 1,000 unfair labor practice case decisions (Table 13). This was about 2,000 cases requiring attention from five persons. Statistics are not kept on interlocutory appeals from judges' and regional directors' rulings on evidence and other points of law. But there were a number of these in addition to the 2,000 cases referred to above. If each Board member took only a two-week vacation and spent no other time out of the office, the member would have available 250 workdays in which to decide these 2,000 cases. This divides out to approximately 8 cases per day to be decided, with a need for a full written decision to issue in approximately one-half of these—1,000 cases, or about four formal written opinions to issue each day.

No backlog developed. The Board did in fact process those 2,000 cases and the unrecorded number of interlocutory matters. The Board also handled its day-to-day administrative duties, which range from minor housekeeping matters to major items such as budget review and the appointment of key personnel such as regional directors and administrative law judges. How did it get all of this done? Obviously by internal delegation and organization, or what may be called a process of assembly line appellate review.

HOW THE ASSEMBLY LINES WORK

One form of internal delegation is the use of three-member panels to decide cases. The five-member Board is authorized, by statute, to act in panels of three, and does so for a sizeable portion of its case load. In all cases other than requests for review, however, the members who do not serve on the panel do review the draft decision prior to its issuance—for "clearance," as it is called. If any nonparticipating member has any problem with the decision, he may request that the case be referred from the panel to the full Board for decision. Thus "true panelization" does not in fact exist, although some Board members rarely exercise their "clearance" privilege and give the cases decided by other panels only the most cursory review. If true

3 Office of Representation Appeals, NLRB.

panelization were used, each Board member's workload would, in theory, be reduced by about two-fifths. For those who make minimal use of their "clearance" rights, the load is probably today at about that level. That still leaves each Board member, however, with about five matters per day to decide and with at least two fully articulated decisions and opinions to issue each workday. As those statistics make clear, more than the panel system is required to handle the case load.

The Board Member's Staff

Board members are authorized by law to be assisted by attorneys assigned to each Board member. Earlier in the Act's history, a "Review Section" had been established by the Board, consisting essentially of a pool of attorneys who assisted the entire Board in the performance of its function. Whatever might be said for the efficiency of such an administrative arrangement, it offended the parties who appeared before the Board. The parties believed that a pool of hired attorneys could too easily assume all of the real decision-making functions of the Board and either ignore the views of presidentially appointed Board members or, in fact, not really ever seek their views. These objections were voiced sufficiently strongly in Congress so that, when the Act was amended in 1947, a prohibition was enacted against the Board's employment, as such, of any attorneys; however, each Board member was permitted to hire an assistant or assistants.[4]

The right to hire assistants has been so fully utilized that some say it has only become a device to restore the old Review Section. Whether that is really true or not, it is true that each Board member today has a staff of approximately twenty attorneys to assist him.

Case Assignment Procedure

Briefly summarized, the process for getting cases decided at the Board is as follows. After the judge's decision, exceptions thereto, and briefs in support of the exceptions have been duly filed with the Board, the Executive Secretary assigns the cases in rotation. That is to say, on one day an allotment of cases ready for assignment will go to one Board member; the next day, another allotment will go to the next Board member, and so on. A rather strict rotational system is maintained to avoid

---

[4] 29 U.S.C. § 144 (1970).

criticism that cases are being deliberately funneled to some member for improper reasons.

When the Board member receives his group of cases, a senior member of his staff assigns each of the cases to a counsel (formerly called legal assistant) who is responsible for reviewing the entire record, including the transcript of the hearing, the exhibits, the administrative law judge's decision, the exceptions, and the briefs. The counsel reports to his supervisor; and between the counsel and the supervisor, a decision is made about whether (a) the case is simple enough so that a draft can be immediately prepared for circulation, or (b) it should go to a "subpanel" for preliminary decision, or (c) a detailed memorandum of law to all the Board members is required.

Most frequently the decision is to send the decision to a "subpanel." The subpanel is composed of a senior staff member from each of three Board members' staffs. Each participant in the subpanel has an opportunity to study the file in advance of any subpanel meeting on the case. At the meeting, the counsel from the "originating" Board member's staff makes a verbal presentation of the case to the subpanel, and the subpanel reaches a tentative decision on how the case should be decided and whether there will be any dissent. It is also within the discretion of the subpanel to decide that the case is too novel or complex for a decision, in which case it will be referred to the full Board. The subpanel may also decide to have the case presented to the panel of Board members for further discussion and decision, but that does not happen very often. Usually, if it remains as a panel case, the counsel from the originating Board member's staff will have the task of preparing a draft decision and circulating it to the panel members for review. Courtesy copies are sent to the nonparticipating Board members so that either of them may request full Board consideration if they desire it. In the course of circulation, some editorial changes may be made, or a Board member may reject the position taken for him by his representative and request further discussion; but more often than not, the draft as circulated, with only minor revisions, is the draft which issues.

Referrals to the Full Board

When a case is referred to the full Board, it is considered at a meeting of the Board called an "agenda." During my term as chairman, we held such agendas on Tuesday and Friday of almost every week, except those weeks in which one or more Board members were out of town and not available. The cases referred to the full Board are likely to be the more complex or novel ones, or ones with issues on which certain Board members have no known positions. Discussions at the Board may be brief or may be quite extensive. Sometimes after lengthy discussion, it becomes apparent that no consensus can be reached, and the case has to be put over to a future agenda when, it is hoped, minds can meet and at least a majority decision can be reached. In the more complex or novel cases, there will be quite frequently as many as four or five separate views. Since it is necessary to get out a majority decision, someone eventually has to yield or a compromise position be struck. In a few cases, to the dismay of the lawyers reading the decisions, different groupings of Board members form separate majorities on the various issues in the case. Opinions written in cases of that kind are difficult to write, difficult to read, and are very confusing to readers looking for reliable precedent.

Once agreement is reached at a full Board agenda on a majority decision, it once again becomes the task of the counsel who was first assigned that case to prepare a draft opinion. Sometimes the same counsel will be assigned the duty of preparing the dissent (if one is required), but more frequently the Board member dissenting will wish to have someone on his own staff prepare the dissenting opinion. And every now and then, a Board member is appointed who writes most of his own dissents. (I did.)

Time Targets

The Board has tried to find ways to keep this assembly line moving. Time targets have been established for the several segments of the above process. Those segments are generally referred to as Stage I, Stage II, and Stage III. Stage I is the time from assignment to subpanel action (or sometimes to the decision to issue a draft without the necessity of taking the case to a subpanel). Stage II is the drafting stage. Stage III is the circulation stage, during which a circulated draft is being reviewed by the various Board members for approval. Once the approval of all Board members has been obtained, there is a final stage, sometimes referred to as the "issuance process," in which the mechanical details of reproduction and the making of necessary docket entries and the like are taken care of before the opinion is released to the parties and, shortly thereafter, to the public.

For the time targets of the various stages to really work, however, rigid self-discipline is required on the part of each Board member. The member must also be an effective administrator over his own staff, making sure that his staff meets the timetables. Close cooperation is also required among all Board members if the targets are to be effectively policed. Those conditions necessary to the effectiveness of the time targets simply do not prevail. I have been able to find no one who could remember any time in the Board's history when they have prevailed. Thus the system breaks down with considerable regularity for a variety of reasons.

BUGS IN THE ASSEMBLY LINE

Many of the problems with the system result from some of the Board members' inabilities, from their staffs' quality and structure, and from the very size of the assembly line. Most important, however, as a source of problems is that there is no single person with the authority to oversee the entire decisional process and to insist upon meeting deadlines. Since each Board member is fully independent and has his own staff, neither the chairman nor any other Board member has any power to control the work habits or patterns of another Board member or his staff. Thus, as can be seen, the assembly line for appellate decision making is a cumbersome one, with no one fully in charge and with much opportunity for slippage.

The Lazy Board Member

First, not all Board members are good self-disciplinarians. If a member is having a problem with a draft decision, such as not being sure whether he agrees with all of it, whether he will request changes in it, or whether he will ask that there be further discussion, the easiest thing to do is to put that case over on a corner of his desk while he reviews others which are easier. Some Board members not only do this regularly, but become artists at doing it. They have learned over time that, if they dispose quickly of easy cases, they can procrastinate on a few difficult ones for quite some time, and their statistical record of median time will still look reasonably good. This can encourage and support some very bad habits. A lazy Board member can delegate to a trusted member of his staff the duty of reviewing the cases for him, with instructions to that staff member to bring to him promptly for signature the decisions in all of the cases which do not require extensive attention. In fact, the lazy Board member can (and sometimes does) simply take his staff member's judgment on those "easy" cases and sign off on them without ever having read any of the papers. If he does this regularly, his record for approving decisions quickly in a large number of cases will be good. Meanwhile, if he procrastinates in getting to those more difficult cases which are brought to him for his careful review, they may sit untended for extended periods of time. Yet his statistical record will not look bad, because his total number of cases will appear satisfactory, and his median time may appear to be excellent.

Meanwhile, the more conscientious Board member who tries to give each case some degree of personal attention and who simply decides each case as it comes to him, spending limited time on the easier cases but more extended time on the more difficult ones, will build a statistical record which does not look nearly as good as that of the lazy member with the contrived *modus operandi* described in the preceding paragraph.

The Poor Administrator

Secondly, not all Board members are good administrators. For the time targets to work, the Board member must enforce those targets on his own staff. If a draft is supposed to be completed within three weeks, the Board member must see to it that every lawyer on his staff knows that three weeks means three weeks. To meet that three-week deadline, each counsel must get his draft to his supervisor well before then so that any difficulties with it can be resolved between him and his supervisor. Then, adequate time must be allowed for the draft to be read by the Board member and for any revisions required by the Board member to be made, edited, and incorporated so that the finished draft can actually start circulating at the end of the three-week period. This requires careful planning and day-to-day coordination. The Board member, his supervisors, and his staff must be disciplined into an established and smoothly operating work pattern.

The Staff

Not all Board members choose a chief counsel who has administrative talents. The chief counsel may instead be selected primarily for his legal ability to deal with complex and difficult labor law issues, rather than for his known ability to administer a staff. To add to the difficulties, each twenty-member staff has a supervisory hierarchy. On each staff, there is a ratio of about one chief for every three or four Indians. The "chiefs," although called supervisors, tend to be editors principally. A draft opinion is originally done by the legal assistant, edited by the assistant's immediate supervisor, fairly frequently edited further by the deputy chief counsel, occasionally once more by the chief counsel, and perhaps by the Board member as well. That can be a lengthy process. The existence of these various levels in the supervisory (or editorial) hierarchy may have resulted, historically, from a conscious effort to have great care go into the editing of each decision. A contributing factor has also been a desire by Board members to maintain a sufficiently ascending order of labor grades within their staffs so that good lawyers will be encouraged to stay with a given Board member. Whatever the cause, the result is a multitiered supervisory structure which, while it may result in some greater attention to quality, inevitably builds more steps—and more time—into the decision-making process.

In most courts, a judge has only one or two clerks. There is thus only one level of editing and/or supervision. The decision goes directly from the clerk to the judge, who may edit or change it, but there are no intervening steps. That was probably once the case at the Board, but not once the big assembly lines developed.

Havens of Inefficiency

The size of the assembly lines also results in havens for inefficient workers. A judge who has only one clerk cannot afford to tolerate a lazy or ineffective assistant. But if he has twenty, it is much easier to tolerate a few incompetent or slow performers; and since the bureaucratic protections against removal are road blocks extremely difficult to hurdle, it becomes even more tempting to tolerate a few drones. Every Board member's staff has them. The big assembly line does breed its own brand of bureaucratic inefficiency.

THE ASSEMBLY LINE'S RECORD OF
PROMPTNESS AND PRODUCTIVITY

The Board's record of timeliness of decisions, insofar as data are available, is set forth in Table 11. Data providing information about the productivity of Board members' staffs are included in Table 12. In computing the average number of cases per staff member in Table 12, I have simply divided the total unfair labor practice and representation decisions issued by the Board by the number of professional employees shown by the records as having been on Board members' staffs in each year. There are, doubtless, more sophisticated ways of measuring productivity, but these calculations give us at least some rough picture of what has been happening.

The Board's record of both timeliness and productivity is very spotty. It shows a good deal less in the way of steady progress than the same data which we examined in chapter V for the timeliness and productivity of the regional offices under the supervision of the General Counsel.

Promptness of Decisions

We have very little data available on timeliness in the early days of the Board's operations. In 1946, however, just prior to the enactment of the first major amendments to the Act, the record is bad. In 1946, it was taking the Board almost 200 days to issue an unfair labor practice case decision and over 80 days to issue an election case decision. Within a few years thereafter, however, the situation was much improved. By 1950, the nearly 200 days for unfair labor practice cases had been reduced to 144 days; and in the election case area, the 82-day figure had been cut to 55 days (Table 11).

In 1951, a remarkable year, the Board decided unfair labor practice cases in a median time of 138 days, and representation cases in a median time of 53 days. The representation case record is extraordinarily good, if one bears in mind that the volume of decisions had increased by that year to 1,609. The Board's total decisions issued in 1951 was 1,904 cases (Table 12). (This appears to be well in excess of the number decided a quarter of a century later in the mid-1970s.)

The large number of cases in the early 1950s occurred because the Board was at that time handling a huge election case load, which rose to the enormously high level of 2,195 in 1953, a number not to be exceeded until the early sixties (1960 and 1961) (Table 12). The 53-day median time for election cases in 1951 was improved upon in 1952 (50 days), and the best record ever was made in 1953 (45 days) (Table 11), a year in which the astoundingly high number of 2,195 such cases was handled. That record of timeliness—45 days—was better than any attained, even by regional directors since the delegation in 1961! According to the 1953 *Annual Report*, the time for handling unfair labor practice cases had also been substantially cut by the end of 1953. Thus, while the chart shows a median time of 161 days, the *Annual Report* states that this was reduced to 116 days by the second half of the year.

That 1953 *Annual Report* makes clear that Chairman Guy Farmer was concentrating upon achieving better time limits for Board decisions, and that he was being highly effective in doing so. The 116-day median for unfair labor practice cases, which the 1953 *Annual Report* says was achieved in the second half of the year, was a lower median than has ever been attained since, except for one year—1966. But by 1966, the representation case time lag had increased from the 45-day level of 1953 to 116 days (Table 11), even though by 1966 the Board was deciding only 157 such cases compared to the nearly 2,000 such cases decided in 1953 (Table 12)!

The 1953 progress, however was short lived. Four years later, in 1957, the unfair labor practice decision time lag was up to nearly 200 days, the worst since 1946 (Table 11). And although the representation case load had dropped from 1953's peak of almost 2,200 cases to only 1,410 contested election cases in 1957, the time lapse had jumped from 45 days in 1953 to 65 days in 1957—an increase of almost 50 percent.

By 1959, however, the year in which Congress authorized the delegation of decision making in election cases to regional directors, 22 days had been cut off the time lapse for unfair labor practice decision making, and the election case time lapse had been cut from 65 days back to 49 days. The Board did not exercise its new discretion to delegate until 1961, and 1962 was really the first year in which it had a major impact. In that year, although the Board decided only about one-quarter as many election cases as it had in 1961 (Table 12), the delay in Board decisions had almost doubled—from 65 days in 1961 to 114 days in 1962 (Table 11)!

Being relieved of a substantial amount of decision-making responsibility in representation cases should, one would think, have enabled the Board staff to devote more time to unfair labor practice cases with a resulting drop in delays there. Some improvement in time lapse in unfair labor practice cases did occur, but it was less than impressive. The time lapse for un- fair labor practice decision making went from 177 days in 1961 to 153 days in 1962. But that 153-day time lapse exceeded that prevailing in 1954 when the election case load had been enor- mously heavier.

The Board's timeliness in representation cases since 1962 has not been good and seems to be getting worse (Table 11). Some modest improvement in 1962's 114-day time lapse was achieved a few years later; but by the end of Chairman McCulloch's chairmanship, the delay had crept back up to nearly 140 days. Another week to ten days has been added to this figure since.

Timeliness in unfair labor practice decisions, however, has improved over 1962's 153-day time lapse. About a month has been cut off of this timetable; and in 1966 (under Chairman McCulloch) and in 1972 (under Chairman Miller), 41 and 37 days, respectively, of improvement can be observed. Neverthe- less, the timeliness was little better in 1975 than it was just over two decades earlier in 1954.

In fairness, however, it must be pointed out that the Board's unfair labor practice case load had more than tripled during those two decades (Table 12). Although the representation case decision-making workload had been substantially reduced, it was the more difficult cases which remained with the Board (rather than being delegated to the regional directors). It is also true that decision making in unfair labor practice cases tends to be more complex and difficult than decision making in election cases.

What appears to have happened, then, is that the Board's staff absorbed a considerable increase in the volume of difficult cases without letting its unfair labor practice case timeliness deteriorate, but also without substantially improving it. The greater complexity of the election cases remaining for decision by the Board seems to have resulted in a substantial increase in time delay there.

Tables 11 and 12, however, also demonstrate a great spotti- ness in the Board's record. There is neither consistent improve- ment nor consistent deterioration. The medians jump around from year to year with no particular relationship to changes in volume or any other observable factor. It is quite a different picture from the relatively steady record of improvement and holding of gains maintained by the regional offices during the last two or three decades.

The Record of Productivity

As for productivity, Table 12 shows that a much larger number of cases processed per staff member existed prior to the 1961 delegation to regional directors of election case decision making. This may have been due to the simpler nature of the representation cases being decided in those years and to the much lower volume of the usually more difficult unfair labor practice work.

On the other hand, one would have expected to find that when the delegation occurred, the Board's staffs would have been cut, since less people should have been required to handle the smaller workload. The data suggest, however, that this did not occur to any substantial degree. The delegation had its first major impact in 1962. For a year or two, Board staffs were slightly reduced, but climbed back to their 1961 strength by 1965. Yet in 1965, a total of only 927 cases were decided by the Board, whereas in 1961 the total had been 2,628! Even some difference in complexity of cases cannot account for the vast difference in productivity between 21 cases per staff member in 1961 and the astoundingly low 6 and 7 cases per staff member which obtained in 1964 and 1965, respectively. Were Board members simply unwilling to reduce their staffs even though the workload has declined? It appears so. Instead they tolerated a situation in which each staff member, on the average, appears to have written only about one full decision every two months!

The productivity of the assembly line did not improve substantially until the 1970s, at which time about a 40 percent productivity increase is evident from the data in Table 12. Even that increase—to a per staff member median of ten cases per year—leaves a good deal to be desired. If, as we have suggested, sixteen cases per year per administrative law judge (Table 9) represents something less than a breakneck pace, then ten cases per year of appellate decision writing is surely snaillike, particularly when one observes that a great many of those decisions are boilerplate forms of one and one-half pages, adopting in full the decisions of the administrative law judges.

THE JUNE RUSH

The rather peculiar behavior of the appellate decision-making assembly line is evidenced in its seasonal pattern of work performance. Table 13 is a month-by-month record of the Board's issuance of decisions in contested unfair labor practice cases from 1940 through 1977 (with incomplete data for a few years). As early as 1945 and 1946, one sees the beginning of a trend toward a concentration of decision issuance in the final quarter of the year. The trend did not develop consistently, however, until the 1960s.

During the latter half of the 1960s, it was at its worst. In 1967, over 43 percent of the Board's total unfair labor practice decisions issued in the last quarter of the year. In both 1969 and 1970, over 42 percent issued in that quarter.

In the 1970s, under my chairmanship, a conscious effort was made to reverse that trend, with some success. The percentage of cases issuing in the last quarter of the fiscal year dropped down into the high 20s and low 30s. Percentages issued in other quarters generally stayed within 5 percentage points from the 25 percent which would mark an even distribution over each of the four quarters. This was a sharp contrast with the worst years of the latter half of the 1960s. In 1967, less than 12 percent of the total decisions were issued in the first quarter; and in 1968, less than 14 percent were issued in that first quarter. In those quarters, productivity must have hit an abysmally low level. Thus, in 1967 when ninety-six decisions issued in the first quarter of the year, there were 121 professional employees on the Board members' staffs. This means that less than one case decision was produced per staff member over a three-month period!

The nature of the patterns which developed, particularly in the 1960s, is made even clearer when we look at the number of June decisions as a percentage of the total decisions issued in unfair labor practice cases in each of the fiscal years. Again, the worst examples appear in the late 1960s. In 1969, almost 25 percent of the Board's decisions for that year issued in June. If the work of the Board had been carried out at a steady pace, only 8.33 percent of the year's decisions would issue in any given month.

The Board obviously fails to manage its case load so as to make steady and maximum utilization of the time of the members and their staffs. These wide cyclical swings also raise some serious quality questions. If, in any industrial plant, the assembly line was regularly turning out two and three times as much product in the last part of the day as it did in the first part, the plant manager would, doubtless, not only conclude that there was severe underutilization of labor in the first part of each workday, but he would also have strong suspicions about the quality of the product being assembled in the later hours of the day. There is, similarly, reason to worry about the quality of the Board's decisions which issue in the June rush.

The reason for the June rush is the Board's effort to meet its projected workload figures by a desperate rush at the end of the fiscal year. Each year it projects for the appropriations committees of the Congress the number of decisions it expects to issue during the year for which the appropriation is sought. If its actual record falls well below this figure, there is fear that the appropriations committees will ask embarrassing questions when the Board comes back for its next appropriation. This fear is a real one for both the presidentially appointed Board members, whose credibility may be put at issue, and their career staffs, whose jobs depend on continued appropriations to support the work of the agency.

Thus when inadequate efforts and poor management during the year leave the Board far short of projections, there follows this rash of decisions in June. But this necessarily means that the cases receive considerably less than usual attention from both staff and Board members. The latter are the most critical. Staff members may have been working on certain cases for considerable periods of time and thus have acquired knowledge of the facts and issues. They may have accumulated a stack of unfinished work on their desks which they then rush to completion—in the form of draft decisions—in June. But when the draft decisions come to the Board members in these great numbers in June, they have probably had little or no previous personal exposure to the cases. Yet, to get the cases out, the Board members must, perforce, approve most of the drafts.

When, as in 1969, 200 unfair labor practice cases issued in June, decisions were issuing at the rate of about ten per workday. The amount of time any given Board member could possibly devote to those cases, while at the same time acting on requests for review in election cases and handling administrative chores, is ridiculously low. It gives real ground for concern about the quality of decisions issued under such circumstances.

The data, although showing some improvement in the early 1970s, have slipped badly again since. In fiscal 1976, under Chairman Murphy, 19 percent of the Board's decisions again issued in June, as compared with the 12 percent June decisions in 1973. The June rush is simply further evidence of a failure by the Board to manage its workload effectively.

The considerable variance in productivity at the Board from both month to month and year to year all suggest the lack of consistent managerial success. Satisfactory administration of the appellate decision-making function has, I fear, not been achieved.

A LOOK AT THE PRODUCT MIX

In looking at an assembly line operation, one of the questions which might well be asked if there were highly irregular variations in both quantity of product and time taken to produce the product would be whether substantial changes in product mix might be responsible. In the Board's case, this is not the cause. The product mix has remained fairly constant; and where there are differing product mixes, there appears to be little correlation with productivity or timeliness.

Unfair Labor Practice Decisions

Table 14 compares, over a three-year period (1972 through 1974), the type of allegations which were acted upon in contested unfair labor practice decisions. It will be seen that the nature of the alleged violations did not alter substantially over this three-year period. Section 8(a)(1) violations, for example, represented 28 percent of the total case load in one year, 32 percent in another, and 30.6 percent in the third year. Section 8(a)(5) violations stayed consistently at approximately 17 percent over the three years. Violations by unions also showed relative constancy in the product mix. Section 8(b)(2) cases represented 5 percent of the total load in 1972, 4 percent in 1973, and 4.7 percent in 1974. Union violations of Section 8(b)(7) stayed very close to the 1 percent level in all three years.

Reversals and Adoptions of
Administrative Law Judges' Decisions

Data supplied by the Executive Secretary of the Board also indicate that, although there were some differences during the four-year period of 1971 through 1974 in the percentages of cases in which administrative law judges' decisions were reversed, the variances do not seem to have had much effect on either productivity or time lag. When the Board adopts the administrative law judge's decision in full, there is virtually no writing at all. The Board has developed a form of one and one-half pages for such adoptions. The Board staff member need do little except fill in a few blanks. On the other hand, when an administrative law judge's decision is reversed, an entirely new opinion fully explicating the Board's differences with the judge must be written and carefully reviewed. This can take substantial time on the part of both staff and Board members.

The easiest cases for the Board—those in which the Board fully adopted the decision of the administrative law judge— ranged from approximately 43 percent of the total Board case load in 1953 to 66 percent in 1971. Yet, time lag in 1971 was the highest of the four years examined (141 days) (Table 11). Time lag in the year of the lowest percentages of those easy cases (1973) was the second lowest of the four years (133 days). Likewise, productivity was at its lowest point for the four years in the year of the greatest percentage of the easy cases (full adoptions). Productivity remained approximately constant during the other three years despite a variance of from 44 percent to 61 percent in full adoptions.[5]

Similarly, the year in which there was the highest percentage of complete or nearly complete reversals of administrative law judges' decisions (over 17 percent in 1974) evidenced no significant increase in time lag (one day) from the prior year when there had been only a 14 percent serious reversal rate.[6] In 1972, however, the time lag was the best achieved during the four-year period. In that year, there was the lowest percentage of serious reversals. But a lack of similar correla-

---

[5] Data on adoptions of ALJ decisions obtained from the Office of the Executive Secretary, NLRB.

[6] Data on reversals of ALJ decisions obtained from the Office of the Executive Secretary, NLRB.

tion in the other years casts doubt on the significance of that one year's statistics.[7]

Dissents

Another variable in product mix which seems worth examination is the proportion of cases in which one or more Board members issued a dissenting view. Dissents take additional member or staff time because of the additional writing and also because the other Board members must review the dissent and determine whether it is necessary for the majority to respond to the dissent. If a response is decided upon, then still further time is required to author and reach agreement upon such a response. It would not be unreasonable to expect, then, that as the proportion of cases in which a dissent is registered increases, staff productivity might tend to decline, and time lags might tend to worsen. The available data, however, do not support such a conclusion.

Thus, in 1974 when dissenting views issued in almost 49 percent of the cases, there was only one day's difference in time lag from 1973, when the number of dissenting views was substantially lower—29 percent.[8] Further, as has been noted before, productivity remained at about the same level in each of those two years, both in total (963 cases—1973; 977 cases—1974) and in average cases per staff member (10 in both years) (Table 12).

Thus, differences in product mix, such as types of law violations alleged, percentages of substantial reversals of administrative law judges' decisions, and cases with and without separate dissenting views, all seem to have had a minimal impact on either timeliness or productivity.

The spottiness of the Board's record of both productivity and timeliness seems, therefore, explicable on no other ground but ineffective and inconsistent administrative management.

WHY THE ASSEMBLY LINE IS BADLY MANAGED

Because the available data tend strongly to indict the Board of ineffective management of its workload, the next logical ques-

---

[7] Data of this kind was not kept by the Office of the Executive Secretary prior to 1971. The total spread of the data is thus so narrow that any conclusions about correlation are tentative at best.

[8] Data on dissenting views obtained from the Office of the Executive Secretary, NLRB.

tion to ask is, Why? Here there is little empirical evidence to draw upon, and I can only record my opinions based almost entirely on my own observations during the four and one-half years in which I served as an NLRB chairman.

Those who worked closely with me at the Board during the term of my chairmanship would all attest that I was acutely interested in improving both the timeliness of Board decisions and the productivity of Board staffs. Different Board chairmen put their emphasis on different areas of the Board's work. Improving the Board's administration of its own case load was one of my primary fields of emphasis, but one in which I encountered enormous frustrations.

While I was successful in substantially improving the productivity of the staffs, I remained totally dissatisfied with the median level of ten cases per staff member per year which we achieved. I was equally disappointed in our inability to achieve any consistent improvement in timeliness of Board decisions. Not only did the median times disappoint me, but I said many times to the Board that it was my goal to reach a point where we had no decision which had lingered at the Board for more than six months. We failed to achieve that end, although we did substantially reduce the number of cases which wore that kind of long beard.

The Tools are Available

In attempting to achieve improved administration in both timeliness and productivity, we used the kinds of tools which most managers use in the private sector to achieve similar goals. By introducing electronic data processing, we were able to provide Board members with prompt and extensive information about where each case was in its progress toward decision, thus supposedly enabling remedial action to be taken on any cases which were lingering longer than they should at any processing stage. We also, through the use of the computer, were able to keep ourselves abreast of the aging of cases and of the number of decisions issuing each week and each day. It seems that we had virtually all of the informational tools which managers need in order to identify problems requiring solution. The advent of that readily accessible data was not totally popular with the staff. Some objections were founded on professional pride which, perhaps legitimately, rejects any claim that a lawyer's professional progress can be measured by machine. Other objections were less worthy, including some from staff supervisors who simply did not want to be bothered about timeliness or productivity and some from staff members whose principal interest seemed to be to keep their own miserable production records as well hidden as possible.

But, despite objections, we did achieve, after working out some initial "bugs," an electronic data storage and retrieval system which worked very well. It did not, however, do the job. The computer was willing, but the flesh was weak.

Indeed, the Board's computer model represented a sort of pilot program for the agency in obtaining prompt information needed for good management. It provided the information so successfully that computer operations were introduced in the Division of Judges. The General Counsel also made some more extensive use of electronic data processing. But because the General Counsel's operations are spread out over the entire country and cover thousands more cases than the appellate case load of the Board, the costs of complete computerization of his information system were much too great to undertake a complete program immediately.

But as is now clear, the computer is not the whole answer to providing good management. The General Counsel has achieved a far better administrative record and continues to maintain it despite the fact that he has far fewer means of automated data reporting than has the decision-making side of the agency.

The Ivory Tower Syndrome

One of the problems of administration in the Board's appellate decision making is a psychological one. Board members and all of their staff members are, in a very real sense, in an ivory tower. They are geographically segregated in a headquarters building on Pennsylvania Avenue in Washington, D.C. They have no daily contact with the employers, unions, and employees who are impatiently awaiting the decisions in their respective cases. This is quite different from the regional office situation where the regional director and all of his staff are daily exposed to the public. Impatient company and union representatives have ready access to the offices and telephones of regional office personnel and do not hesitate to complain loudly if their cases are not being promptly investigated or otherwise acted upon. Not so at the Board.

For the Board, the separation is geographic and more. In order that neither the Board nor their staffs may be subjected to improper pressures, no Board member will talk with any party to a case awaiting decision. For the same reasons, the identity of the staff members working on any particular case is carefully controlled information, not released to the public and certainly not released to the parties. The Executive Secretary's office and the secretaries on Board staffs are all carefully trained to keep any callers away from Board members and their staffs in order to avoid such undesired pressures.

This isolation is healthy in the judicial sense. During the Watergate years, there was reason to be glad that the Board had so effectively insulated itself that there could never be— and never was—a single accusation of improper pressures ever having been exerted on the NLRB members or staffs. But while such insulation is effective in avoiding political and partisan pressures, it is also effective in removing Board members and their staffs from a true appreciation of the urgency of the tasks at hand. The human reality of the conflicts and disputes involved in the cases are not impressed upon the minds of these insular participants in the appellate decision-making process. All that the Board members or lawyers working for them ever see of these realities are the cold transcripts and the frequently dull briefs filed by lawyers for the parties. Into that kind of environment, a sense of urgency rarely penetrates.

This means, in turn, that all deadlines are self-imposed and appear artificial. The incentive to meet those deadlines is thereby diminished. The practicing attorney facing a deadline for a brief knows that, if he wants to win his case, he had better get that case to the judge by the day set or the judge will never read his arguments. The Board member or the staff member who does not get the draft decision circulated the day it was supposed to have been circulated faces no such consequences. It just issues later; and if it issues early, well, the stack of cases to work on is one case lighter. So?

It is thus difficult in the Board's decisional ivory tower to instill any realistic sense of urgency of the kind which motivates human beings to take prompt and effective action.

The Weak Links in the Chain

Never have I seen so dramatically demonstrated the truth of the old saw that a chain is only as strong as its weakest link. As might be expected, some Board members are better administrators than others. Some Board members are more interested in achieving both promptness and efficiency than are others; and, of course, some Board members are better self-disciplinarians than others. But it takes only one slow, disinterested, lazy, preoccupied, or indecisive Board member to effect a significant slowdown in the progress of any case or group of cases.

From time to time, it has been suggested that the decisions of the Board ought, like appellate court decisions, to disclose the name of the author of the opinion. (This is what is said. What is meant in the context of the real world at the NLRB is that the author shown would be the Board member on whose *staff* the text of the opinion was written. With the present volume of cases, almost no majority opinions are personally authored by a Board member himself.) One of the reasons proffered for the suggestion is that it might embarrass a Board member if he were shown to be the author of an opinion which took too long to issue.

This suggestion fails to take into account how the Board really operates. Delays can be and are as effectively caused by a Board member's failure to act on a circulating draft as they are by a failure to circulate a timely draft. Since information about which Board member is responsible for holding up a case at any stage is not made available to the public, the identification of the "author" of an opinion would, more often than not, embarrass the author unfairly and fail to be helpful in disclosing the true source of the delay.

Inefficient or inattentive conduct on the part of any one Board member can not only have a direct impact on the progress of a case, but it also tends to impede the administrative effort of all other Board members. Thus, if one Board member does not insist that his staff members circulate draft opinions in cases assigned to his staff within the due dates that are established, members of other staffs feel extraordinarily put upon if their Board member requires them to adhere to targets which can be so easily ignored elsewhere. Or, if a Board member allows a case to sit on the back of his desk for weeks or even months, as is sometimes the case, any urging by the Board or the

Board members or by the chairman that a staff member improve his timeliness rings hollow. The staff members know too well the delinquencies of certain Board members and see little point in rushing to complete drafts when the last several they completed have been awaiting action for unseemingly long periods. So the weakness of one link is not only fatal: it is contagious.

It is easy for any Board member who is less conscientious than others to cover up successfully his lack of concern about promptness and efficiency. If opinions authored on his staff are promptly acted upon by other Board members even though circulated late, and if other Board members circulate cases promptly but the cases are not acted on promptly by the delinquent Board member, the statistics at the end of the year will indicate that the total time for cases originating from his staff compares well with that for cases originating from any other Board member's staff. Furthermore, if he is a truly lazy Board member and delegates to his staff the authority to approve all of the easy cases, but sits unconscionably long on the hard ones, the median time for his staff will still look very good.

What one weak link in the chain of Board members can do, a weak link in staff efficiency can do as well. Because the volume of cases on which Board action is required has grown so large, each Board member is, as we have already pointed out, greatly dependent on the work and recommendations filtered up to him by his staff. If the staff is slow in making those recommendations or slow in performing the writing chores required of them, there will be a weakness in the chain. Since discharge of government employees is extraordinarily difficult to effectuate, a Board member saddled with a number of inefficient, unproductive, or slow lawyers on his staff is nearly powerless to take any effective action to correct the situation. In theory, the staffs of Board members are not subject to the usual Civil Service rules, but the Board some years back, in an act of magnanimity, conferred like privileges upon these employees. Those privileges are now firmly embedded as part of their working conditions, particularly since most of the staff is now represented by a government-employee labor organization.

The carrot of within-grade increases, Sustained Superior Performance awards, and the like can be used to motivate many staff lawyers to improve their performance. But each Board staff has some underachievers who cannot be motivated by such means. They have learned that they can produce very little and still retain their jobs. They are seriously weak links in the case-processing chain.

Nevertheless, by using the available motivational techniques, a conscientious Board member interested in good administration can, to a considerable extent, succeed in getting his staff to achieve reasonably good productivity and timeliness records. Board members who have formerly served as regional directors have a well-deserved reputation for being able to achieve just such success on their respective staffs. This is proof of the pudding. But just one Board member who is not as skillful and as experienced an administrator will supply the weakness in the chain and ruin the record of the entire Board. Since the appointment of five able administrators at any one time to the Board would be a remarkable coincidence, the weak link is almost always there.

The Bureaucratic Layers

Another factor which impedes both timeliness and efficiency is the heavy overlay of supervisory levels within each Board's staff. Each Board's staff has a chief counsel, a deputy chief counsel, three supervisors (now called special counsel), together with approximately fifteen nonsupervisory attorneys. Thus, when in Table 12 we compute an average of ten cases per staff member for fiscal years 1972-1974, we are not being quite fair to the nonsupervisory attorney. Because only about two-thirds of the Board's staffs are nonsupervisory, the nonsupervisory attorney can claim that he actually handles a median of fifteen cases. Yet the true overall productivity rate is only ten per staff member, because supervisory, as well as nonsupervisory, attorneys are involved in the issuance of every decision. And the truth is that if a nonsupervisory staff member is really weak (and some are), the supervisor has to redo his or her work so fully that the supervisor really must be regarded as a "relief operator" as well as, or even more than, a supervisor.

It is questionable whether this much supervision is required over the decision-writing functions of the Board's staff members. Should each draft decision really go to a supervisor, then to the deputy chief, and sometimes to the chief before being submitted to the Board member? Is there that much improvement in quality achieved by this route? Should even routine affirmances of administrative law judges' decisions go through this many hands? Why cannot any full affirmance go directly to a Board member for approval?

The practical difficulty with this latter suggestion, which would eliminate one or two steps for every full adoption, is that it would be resisted, perhaps not openly, because it would require the Board member to read the administrative law judge's decision and the briefs of the parties and actually make up his own mind. Some Board members prefer to leave this kind of work to their trusted supervisors; and, if assured by the supervisors that the case is routine and that the administrative law judge seems to have decided the issues correctly, many a Board member will simply "sign off" on the case without reading the decision of the administrative law judge which is being affirmed.

Although it may be argued that the quality of decision making is maintained by requiring the case to go through so many staff levels of supervision, there can be no doubt that additional delay is caused thereby. The duplication of work also necessarily decreases the productivity of the staff. Furthermore, the all too comforting assurance that so many people have already reviewed the file offers a less conscientious Board member a convenient rationale for shirking his duty to study the cases personally.

Time and efficiency are also lost because opinions tend to be overedited. A supervisor may change the originating lawyer's draft for real reasons of quality or merely because he prefers a different style. It is very difficult in many instances to distinguish between the two. The next level of supervision may redo the same draft, again partially for reasons of style; so may the next level of supervision; and if the Board member is also concerned about the manner and style of the writing, he may make still further changes. These multiple revisions may be of dubious value in terms of the real substance of the decision.

This heavy supervisory overlay also increases the opportunities for "weak links" in the chain. Just one supervisor in the process who is slow, who may be ill, who grows weary of the task as he ages, or who for any reason fails to do his job efficiently can add days and weeks to the delay in any individual case.

Other complexities built into the case-processing system offer the same kinds of opportunities for human failure. With each human being that is added to the process comes one more chance for failure, delay, and procrastination.

Take, for example, the subpanel technique, wherein trusted staff members from three staffs arrive at tentative decisions. Such a procedure "works" only if the staff members cast a vote at the subpanel meeting which accurately reflects each of their respective member's true view. If it turns out that a Board member's representative did not properly reflect his views, then all the work that went into a draft may have to be undone, causing expenditures of time that would not have been necessary had the Board members themselves personally participated in the first discussion.

An unduly cautious subpanel member may ask, on behalf of his member, that a detailed legal memorandum be written on the case although in fact the Board member would not have needed such a memorandum and would have been ready to vote immediately on the issues. The opportunity for such relatively easy-to-make miscalculations occur every time a staff member is forced by the system to guess at his Board member's view. Every such miscalculation costs time and results in duplication or unnecessary expenditure of effort.

Thus, although these extra internal structures have been adopted in an effort to enable the Board to cope with a volume of work which has grown too large for a five-person Board, they have also resulted in cumbersome structures which frequently function less than perfectly and thus adversely affect both timeliness and productivity.

At the hands of a "weak link" Board member, these structures become even more of a problem. The Board member who will not take the time and trouble to keep his staff clearly advised of his views on issues makes it virtually impossible for his subpanel representative to do an effective job. Delays will be inevitable because the staff member was unable to anticipate his member's view properly. The Board member who does not have a sufficiently disciplined staff will soon have subpanel representatives who do not prepare in advance for subpanel meetings, or who may not even appear at the meeting, thus wasting the time of the entire subpanel. Thus, once again, the internal mechanisms designed to help with the growing case load easily founder on the imperfections of just one Board member. Every other Board member may be an excellent administrator, but all can be at the mercy of only one colleague who is wanting in administrative capacity or desire.

Where is the Boss?

Because responsibility for the tasks involved in making and articulating decisions is not centralized in any single administrator, but is dispersed among five equals, effective administration by the Board is indeed almost an impossibility.

While the Board has a chairman, the chairman has no authority over the other Board members, except as they may wish to confer it voluntarily. Generally, the Board members are cooperative in deferring to the chairman in many administrative matters and permit the chairman to act without prior consultation on some administrative matters. Nevertheless, they are understandably jealous of their prerogatives and of their authority as presidential appointees. In some agencies headed by such a multiperson Board, the hiring of even the lowest grade employee must be approved by all Board or commission members. The NLRB has shown better sense than to allow such ridiculous practices to prevail and has avoided much internal conflict by delegating substantial administrative authority to the General Counsel. The fact that this delegation to the General Counsel can be quickly withdrawn if the Board really disapproves of his action permits the Board to feel that it still has authority. But on a day-to-day basis, it thus avoids the pitfalls of administration by committee.

Where the operations of the immediate Board staffs are involved, however, no such centralization exists. The chairman manages his staff, and each other Board member manages his own. The Executive Secretary's office is allowed to operate with only limited independence. Board members insist upon taking an active role in who is appointed to even very junior professional and semiprofessional positions in the Executive Secretary's office. I once attempted to get my colleagues to vest in the Executive Secretary the authority to make all such appointments on his own, or to permit me to make them as chairman. They refused. Although the Board is willing to delegate to the General Counsel the right to make appointments in the regional offices, this was too close to home.

Yet this very absence of delegation and the resultant scheme of decentralized authority renders ineffective the Board's administration of its own work, leaving the management of its case load totally vulnerable to the weakest link and frustrating all efforts at the kind of effective administration which it has been possible for the General Counsel's side of the agency to attain.

There is some truth to the quip that a camel is a horse built by a committee. The decision-making apparatus of the Board lumbers along much more like a camel than a race horse.

CONCLUSIONS

To revert to our original metaphor, if there were only one assembly line in the Board's appellate decision making, it might function well; however, five assembly lines which are inter-dependent but which are each autonomously managed can be all too easily jammed by the slightest malfunction in any one of the lines.

Does assembly line appellate review work? Well, it gets the Board's increasingly large volume of cases decided; but personal Board member participation has been substantially diluted, and a cumbersome multiheaded bureaucracy has been built which has no solid record for achieving a significantly success-ful record of either productivity or timeliness. A better decision-making process seems much needed.

CHAPTER VIII

When the Board Goes to Court

The Board can order companies and unions to cease and desist from the kinds of improper activities in which it has been found they engage and to take certain affirmative action to remedy violations found. But the Board has no authority, on its own, to enforce those orders. Instead, the statute provides that it must go to a court of appeals of the United States judiciary and seek to have that court enforce its orders. Or, a company or a union found guilty by the Board of having committed a violation may petition a court of appeals to review the Board's findings and to set aside the Board order. In either event—which is to say, in all those cases in which the respondents do not voluntarily comply with the Board order— the matter will reach a federal appellate court. If the court enforces the order and the respondent fails to comply with the court order, the Board may have to go back to court to institute contempt proceedings.

THE DIVISION OF ENFORCEMENT LITIGATION

The Board also must go to court as a result of other miscellaneous litigation, such as suits brought against the Board under the Freedom of Information Act and suits to enjoin the Board from taking action alleged to be beyond its jurisdiction or to force it to take action alleged to be required of it by law. In order to handle the appellate litigation and this variety of miscellaneous litigation, the Board maintains a special staff, known as the Division of Enforcement Litigation, in its headquarters in Washington, D.C.[1] Again, in the interest of ef-

---

[1] The statute also authorizes and sometimes mandates that the Board seek injunctive relief against certain kinds of law violations even before the matter has been fully litigated before the Board. Those injunction proceedings were once handled out of the Washington staff which handles appellate litigation. This is no longer so, except in unusual cases. Such injunctive relief is now normally sought by lawyers working in the Board's regional offices.

ficient administration, the direction of that staff has been entrusted by the Board to the General Counsel. Until recent years, however, it tended to operate as a nearly autonomous unit. The division has a high *esprit de corps*, and the lawyers who work therein regard themselves as an elite group, as indeed they are. Some of the brightest young minds recruited from law schools are assigned to this work, and the only applicants from within the agency who successfully obtain transfers to this division are those with exceptionally good records and recommendations. There can be no denying that the division houses a group of able, bright, and intelligent lawyers.

The Division's Promptness

The administration of the division, however, for many years left a good deal to be desired, and current statistics suggest that still further improvement could yet be achieved. Until just a few years ago, a case could easily remain in the Division of Enforcement Litigation for many months, and even occasionally for years, while one or more of this group of skilled lawyers carefully drafted, redrafted, and massaged every phrase in the brief to the appellate court. The briefs were often excellent, but the delays from all this careful rewriting and reediting resulted in the same kind of injustice which delays anywhere in the course of the proceeding can and do cause.

But the delay here was further compounded by the fact that the appellate courts have, in recent years, tended to have clogged calendars. This meant that a case might sit in the Board's Division of Enforcement Litigation for as long as a year and then, once filed, could well sit in a court of appeals for at least another year. While, therefore, the General Counsel was successfully pushing his field staffs to meet thirty-day or forty-five-day time targets in moving cases along, the respondents who chose to litigate all the way could count on additional years on the route to an enforceable order.

In more recent years, particularly after Peter Nash was named as General Counsel, very serious attention was paid to this delay problem. As a result, cases are being filed in the courts of appeals within a median time of thirty to sixty days after it becomes evident that a respondent is not going to comply with a Board decision.[2] That is a spectacularly better schedule than prevailed in the decades preceding General Counsel Nash's appointment.

The benefits accruing to respondents by delaying compliance with Board orders have thus been minimized, and compliance with Board orders without resort to the courts has thus been substantially encouraged. The data in Table 1 show that the percentage of cases in which compliance with Board decisions has been obtained without resort to litigation has dramatically increased over what it was, even as recently as 1965. As that table indicates, the percentage of such voluntary compliance was running between 42 and 44 percent of cases in the mid-1960s, whereas it is now up to 68.6 percent in 1975. It will be noted that a level of voluntary compliance in the 60 percent range was not obtained until 1973, which almost coincides with the time at which the great improvement in promptness in getting to the courts was effectuated. It seems that taking some of the delay out of the enforcement process may have persuaded many respondents that it was not worthwhile to contest the matter on into the courts.

Yet courts of appeals continue to have crowded dockets; and even though the division gets to court promptly, the court itself will take approximately a year (median time) to issue its decision. So the delay to enforceable order is still substantial.

The Record of Productivity

Productivity in the litigation area also continues to suggest that too much "jewelry work" is still being done on briefs, even though petitions for enforcement are being more promptly filed. We have seen that an administrative law judge or a member of the staff of a Board member handles only a dozen (or sometimes less) cases a year—a figure which seems very low to any busy practitioner. In enforcement litigation the productivity data are equally disturbing, showing a median productivity of seven or eight briefs filed per professional per year in appellate litigation (Table 15).

A private practitioner would doubtless find a workload consisting solely of writing seven or eight appellate briefs a year a pretty lei-

---

[2] In 1973—fifty-seven days; 1974—thirty-five days; 1975—thirty-four days; 1976—thirty-eight days. Data supplied by the Office of the Executive Secretary, NLRB.

surely schedule. It does not evidence truly effective use of lawyers' time or of taxpayers' money.

There has been some improvement in recent years. Under General Counsel Peter Nash, the 6.6 briefs filed for staff year 1970 increased to 8.2 in 1973. While there was some deterioration after that, the figure under General Counsel Irving has now increased to 8.4. Despite this improvement, the quantity of briefs written by each lawyer remains unimpressive, at least to this author.

The quality of the Board's appellate litigation efforts is of very real importance, and it should not be allowed to deteriorate or be ignored in the interest of economy. But it seems that high quality could be maintained with a greater productivity rate than that which now obtains, even though substantial improvement in this area has already been made. The elite corps of enforcement attorneys can do better, and there is good reason to believe that much of this appellate work could more efficiently be handled by the regional offices.

An experiment in this area was carried out in 1971; as chairman, I and then General Counsel Ordman agreed to farm out a few appellate cases to the regions. The results were quite satisfactory, but perhaps the best result was an indirect one—note that the 1972 productivity shown in Table 15 is nearly 25 percent higher than that of 1970. There can be little doubt but that this substantial increase was due in part at least to a fear that greater use would be made of field personnel for this work.

There are many who say that the experiment should not have been discontinued, even though the elite corps at headquarters pleaded urgently for retaining the work and did achieve substantial productivity improvements. If the present outmoded statutory structure of the Board is allowed to continue, and the work of enforcing Board orders in the courts must still be undertaken in a substantial number of cases, further experimentation in assigning cases to the field would be a good morale builder in the field offices and would provide useful comparative data by which to judge productivity.

DELEGATING ROUTINE APPEALS TO
FIELD PERSONNEL

The intense need for centralized and highly specialized appellate lawyers has diminished in some degree since the early days of the Act. Difficult and vitally important issues, such as those dealing with the constitutionality of the Act and first principles of administration and interpretation, arise less frequently today then they did when the Act was new. During those tentative days, it was important to have the appellate staff working under the very close supervision of a centralized supervisory staff. Uniformity and internal consistency in approach to such fundamental issues was essential. Today much of the appellate litigation is of an almost routine nature, and there is much less justification for complete centralization. The attorneys in the regional offices who have handled the investigation and trial of the matter before the administrative law judge and written the briefs during the appeal to the Board have acquired a complete knowledge of the case. They should be able to handle the court review more efficiently than a lawyer in Washington who is new to the case and who must therefore spend substantial time familiarizing himself with all of the facts and the applicable law.

There seems little reason, therefore, not to delegate much of the appellate court work to attorneys in the field. A small staff could be retained in Washington to handle cases involving novel, complex, or particularly important issues on which both extra care and ready access to the General Counsel or his top assistants may be necessary or at least desirable. By thus using field personnel for most of the cases and a small, centralized "elite corps" for the potentially precedent-setting ones, it would seem that productivity and efficiency could be substantially improved.

True, there would be potential morale problems created by reducing a staff of well over fifty lawyers to perhaps five or ten. Bureaucratic restrictions also impede such drastic changes. But since the Board's field offices are particularly short of trained, skilled, legal talent, there ought to be ample opportunity for regional placement of the lawyers no longer needed in a centralized appellate litigation section. For those interested in private practice, the Bar is normally very interested in lawyers with experience in the Division of Enforcement Litigation because of that division's reputation for employing top-notch lawyers. Thus the proposed reduction in this work force should be less of a problem than most such cutbacks.

While a change of that nature could improve the efficiency of the Board's appellate court work, the basic problem of delay caused by the cumbersome structure of the statutory scheme would remain. For the statute requires that two appeals—one

to the Board and one to a federal appellate court—must follow
the trial judge's decision before that decision has any authority.
The first appeal, at the Board level, consumes about four or
five months, and the second, at the court level, consumes another year or more. That long road is at the heart of the problem of effective enforcement of the NLRA. Until it is solved—
and it can only be solved by a statutory change in the decision-
making structure—the Board's function as public law enforcer
cannot be efficiently or effectively administered.

CHAPTER IX

The NLRB and the Dollar Sign

When we take a quick measure of the importance and effectiveness of a private sector institution, it is common to think in terms of dollar signs. Is it a company with a million-dollar sales volume or a billion-dollar sales volume? Is it a money maker or a money loser? And one key of the businessman's evaluation of a manufacturing facility is whether it has a history of and a continuing potential for producing at a decreasing unit cost.

Even in the nonprofit segment of the private sector, one often asks about the size of the annual budget and how many people the institution serves. Increasingly, also, we look at "unit cost" there. The public wants to know how much of its contributions are going to the intended beneficiaries of the charity, and how many dollars are being eaten up by administrative costs.

But in government, it is less common to think in those terms. The task force appointed by former Chairman Murphy of the NLRB issued a lengthy report which, if I have not missed something, contains not one single dollar sign.

Yet there are at least two measuring areas in which dollar signs may be of interest in trying to make some kind of administrative evaluation of the NLRB. The first area is overall "unit cost" to the taxpayers, and the second is "unit cost" in relation to the dollar volume of reimbursements ordered by the NLRB to remedy economic losses caused by law violations.

OVERALL UNIT COST

Looking first at taxpayer costs, there are perhaps two questions we can try to answer: Is the overall cost of the agency becoming an undue burden on the taxpayer? Is the unit cost of case handling getting out of hand or remaining well under control?

The first inquiry will, doubtless, have primarily subjective answers, and calls for underlying value judgments. That does not mean the area is not worth exploring, or the question not worth asking. Each citizen for himself, or at least the citizenry as a whole acting through the Congress, surely ought to make periodic judgments about whether the contribution to society made by each of our governmental, tax-supported organizations is worth its cost. Is the NLRB, in carrying out its functions as an honest ballot association and as a public law enforcer, worth the total cost to the taxpayers? That cost is substantial, although it is relatively modest by current governmental fiscal standards. As indicated in Table 16, the cost to the taxpayers is now over $68 million per year. That cost also seems steadily to rise. Table 16 shows that, from a modest beginning in 1936, at an annual cost of a little over $600,000, the dollar signs had quintupled and exceeded the $3 million mark as early as 1940. They quintupled again to $15 million by 1960, exceeded $25 million by 1965, and more than doubled again in the next decade.

The Increase in Cost and Cases

The fundamental reason for the increased costs is easily discoverable by a quick glance at the column in Table 16 showing numbers of cases. The total number of cases increased tenfold from 1936 to 1940 and has continued to grow steadily throughout the Board's history. So, too, however, has the cost of processing each one of them grown in, almost but not quite, every year. The average cost per case has more than tripled since 1940.

Yet the data do not indicate that the agency has become more wasteful. We cannot evaluate these data without taking into account the diminishing buying power of the dollar.

The cost of living index (all items—1967 equals 100) increased from 42.0 in 1940 to 170.5 in 1976, thus indicating that inflation has brought costs more than four times as high in 1976 as in 1940.[1] But costs per case in 1976 were only 3.4 times as high as in 1940, thus reflecting a decreasing unit cost in real dollars.

When one considers the substantial improvement which has been made over those years in the speed with which cases are handled, and when one bears in mind all of the added burdens heaped on governmental administrators through increasing external regulation of the affairs of those agencies, it is rather remarkable that costs appear to have been kept so well in line. It seems particularly remarkable if we recognize that bottom line figures are not the *raison d'être* of this or any other govern-

---

[1] 1 BNA 1977 Collective Bargaining Negotiations and Contracts, at 10:126.

mental institution, and that cost consciousness is rarely a bureaucratic hallmark.

If history is any guide, we can expect continuing rising costs, growing primarily out of ever-increasing case loads. Nobody really knows why that case load keeps jumping. It is amusing to read through past statements made by agency chairmen and General Counsels to the congressional appropriations committees. For years it was the fashion to include in those annual appeals for funds an attempted analysis of why the Board's case load kept increasing. Reasons ranged all the way from fatalism— what Frank McCulloch called the "inevitable expansion of the Board's jurisdiction"—to the more fashionable buzz words, such as "population explosion." [2] An estimated reduction in the rate of the case rise was attributed to the Viet Nam war, but that estimation had to be quickly withdrawn in 1969 and confessed as an error in projections.[3]

Frank McCulloch's statement before the House Appropriations Committee on February 11, 1964, provides a more extensive example of the difficulty of explaining the Board's burgeoning case load:

> We have often been asked the question, "Why does the Agency's intake keep rising each year no matter whether the dominant economic pattern in the Country is prosperity or recession?" I think the answer is that in large measure the Agency's work intake depends on the factor of change in economic activity rather than a distinct or predominant pattern in one direction or another.
>
> If an area is growing economically, there will be new plants, more workers, and labor organizing activity; this will result in representation filings and related unfair labor practice cases. It is important to note that this type of economic activity brings both types of filings.
>
> On the other hand, an area which is threatened by loss of jobs brings struggles to protect job rights and, when jobs are actually lost, charges of discrimination. Here it should be noted that unfair labor practice filings are prevalent with few representation petitions.

---

[2] *Hearings on Dep'ts of Labor and Health, Education, and Welfare Appropriations for 1962 Before a Subcomm. of the House Comm. on Appropriations,* 87th Cong., 1st Sess., at 477 (1961); *Hearings on Dep'ts of Labor and Health, Education, and Welfare Appropriations for 1966 Before a Subcomm. of the House Comm. on Appropriations,* 89th Cong., 1st Sess., at 62 (1965).

[3] *Hearings on Dep'ts of Labor and Health, Education, and Welfare Appropriations for 1968 Before a Subcomm. of the House Comm. on Appropriations,* 90th Cong., 1st Sess., pt. 1, at 820 (1967).

Since our Country really consists of many, many small industrial areas and a smaller number of large industrial areas,
conflicting forces are always at work, even in single areas, giving rise to both types of circumstances.

Although we are aware that each of these circumstances gives
rise to case filings, it is very difficult, if not impossible, to fore-
tell what will happen in any one area in the next fiscal year,
let alone in the Nation as a whole.[4]

In other words, the Board's case load has continued to increase
in times of prosperity, in times of recession, in times of peace,
and in times of war because economic flux and the country's industrial and economic variety create situations, good and bad,
in which the Board will become involved. As McCulloch acknowl-
edges, this is not a satisfactory or adequate answer by which we
can fully understand or accurately measure the growth of the
Board's case load.

Another reason, however, perhaps the underlying reason, is
that the Board is simply there, its very existence inviting its use
as a tactical tool in collective bargaining. With the growth of
unionism, the standing and ensuing struggles between labor
and management have become increasingly sophisticated; and
the Board, in its legislated purpose, on the one hand, and its
bureaucracy, on the other, simultaneously offers a legitimate
solution to labor relations disputes and a threat and obstacle
to that solution. No one, however, understands all of the reasons for the increase, and history demonstrates that the case load
does indeed keep going up. Costs seem always to continue to rise,
and there can be no assurance that unit costs will be as well controlled as they have been. Although during my term as chairman,
in at least two fiscal years, substantial monies were returned to
the Treasury when the predicted case load did not develop, there
is no prior history of that kind of financial management, nor can
one reasonably expect it to recur frequently in this or any
other government agency. The cost of regulation will go up.

Is the holding of elections in ever smaller units of employees
and the function of law enforcement by a public prosecutor
worth over $1,500 or more for each charge and each election
petition? If so, is there a cost per case which is more than the
public is willing to pay? Those judgments must be made by the
Congress and by informed voters who elect the Congress. It will

---

[4] *Hearings on Dep'ts of Labor and Health, Education, and Welfare Appropriations for 1965 Before a Subcomm. of the House Comm. on Appropriations,*
88th Cong., 2d Sess., at 64 (1964).

probably not receive dramatic attention, because the overall agency budget is not staggering and amounts to only around $.30 per person.[5] But the questions nevertheless seem worth asking.

UNIT COST AND REIMBURSEMENT

The second unit cost inquiry is the cost per dollar of reimbursement achieved by the Board for wrongs done to individuals by by those companies and unions which violate the law. These cases comprise the bulk of the Board's case load and include hearings on violations by employers, by unions, or by the two acting in concert, such as wrongs of discrimination in employment, coercion of employees, or causation of wage losses. When such violations are found, the Board attempts to remedy that wrong by restoring the *status quo* and making the employee whole for at least the wage losses he or she has suffered, but normally leaving items of other damages to be resolved by the courts. Backpay awards are thus some measure of the effectiveness with which the Board does remedy proven or admitted unfair labor practices. Another measurement may also be the number of employees who are found to have lost their jobs through discrimination on account of union or antiunion activity and who, under the Board's aegis, are offered reinstatement. Table 17 provides information on those cases in which employer violations were remedied through offers of reinstatement and/or through backpay.

Reinstatement Offers

Table 17 deserves some study. It shows, for example, that there has been a real decrease in jobs and wages lost because of wrongs committed against employees. In the early years covered by the table (1939 to 1942), over 180,000 employees were offered reinstatement, a far greater number than during any quadrennial period thereafter. Except for one unusual year (1959, in which over 42,000 were offered reinstatement), the total number of reinstatement offers never exceeded 10,000 after 1942. In all but six years since 1942, the total has been less than 5,000. Although the fact that discrimination seems regularly to occur in from 3,000 to 5,000 cases every single year is not heartening,

---

[5] This calculation is based on a population estimate of 216,376,000 taken from U.S. DEP'T OF COMMERCE, BUREAU OF THE CENSUS, SER. P-25 POPULATION ESTIMATES AND PROJECTIONS No. 702 (May 1977).

the improvement over the nearly 60,000 such instances in 1939 is dramatic.

Many employees choose not to accept reinstatement or to waive reinstatement before it is ever formally offered, but do accept backpay as a partial remedy. This is regarded by some as a failure of the Act, since it shows, arguably, that the *status quo* has not really been restored. It is thus frequently alleged that the employer who flagrantly discriminates may in fact rid himself of union activists merely for the price of the backpay. That is not really true, and furthermore it is somewhat unrealistic to expect that an employee will rush back to a job where he is not wanted, whether his employer's reasons for not wanting him are good or bad, lawful or unlawful. Going back to work for an employer is not pleasant when acceptance of the reemployment has been forced on a hostile employer by a government agency. Indeed, European nations do not understand how we make reinstatement work at all, and the laws of very few other countries even attempt it. But that is an aside.

Backpay

The number of employees receiving backpay has ranged from as low as 1,196 in 1948 to over 15,000 in 1966. There seem to be no clear trends or patterns, except that the numbers have hovered around the 6,000 and 7,000 marks in most years in the last decade. The total dollar amount of backpay also varies considerably, again without symmetry of pattern. Dollars of reimbursement have ranged from a low of around $400,000 to highs in 1975 and 1976 of over $11 million.

The average backpay per employee has tended to increase over the years. This may, in part, be attributable to inflation, but the data suggest that something more than mere inflation is at work. During 1939 through 1942, average backpay per employee was about $200. In more recent years, it has stayed closer to the $1,000 mark. Comparing 1940 with 1976, we see inflationary cost increases of a little over 300 percent, but average backpay increases here of over 600 percent.

AGENCY COSTS—ARE THEY JUSTIFIED?

The relationship between taxpayer cost and money reimbursed by law violations to victims of discrimination is also of interest (Table 18). In 1976, the taxpayers' cost was almost $6 per every dollar of recovery of backpay for wronged employees. In

1970, the taxpayer paid over $14 in agency support money for each dollar recovered by a wronged employee. Each of those years is a far cry from the 1940 record of over $2 million in backpay recovered for employees at a cost to the taxpayers of $1.50 per dollar recovered.

The annual per dollar costs vary, with no clear pattern discernible from an examination of Table 18. But the absence of any such pattern suggests that the agency's costs are not particularly related to remedying specific monetary losses for individual employees, and that its costs are not and cannot be geared to suit recoveries. If the agency's costs are to be justified, it would seem they must be justified on the values of total regulation rather than on the basis of recoveries of damages for employees.

The effect of the total regulation on the nation's economy may be significant, but the dollars recovered for individual employees are by no means increasing proportionately to the increase in the size of the agency or the cost of maintaining it. The significance of that decreasing ratio and the value of increasing regulatory cost to accomplish other less tangible results on all matters brings us back again to the basic judgment which Congress and the American public must make.

As we move into an era when even the political party which has traditionally favored more governmental regulation seems to be rethinking its views about that and about regulatory costs, and even looking for some areas in which deregulation can be experimented with, perhaps these much neglected dollar sign and unit cost measurements ought to be brought to the foreground. Surely they ought at least to be one of the factors taken into account when trying to assess the worth of this and other regulatory agencies.

CHAPTER X

The NLRB—How Can We Make It Work Better?

Thus far we have taken a look at the various segments of the NLRB's operations—the honest ballot association, the General Counsel's Threshing Machine, the administrative (but unadministerable) law judges, the Assembly Line For Appellate Decision Making, and the Long Road to the Court House—viewing them all with the aim of seeing what functions are involved in trying to make the National Labor Relations Act work and of evaluating, to a degree at least, how efficiently or inefficiently and how expensively or inexpensively the present machinery works. All of that description and evaluation would seem purposeless if, at this point, we did not pay some attention to what might be done to make the machine work better.

THE ADVANTAGES AND DISADVANTAGES OF PAST CHANGES

It must be remembered, first of all, that the machinery is now over forty years old, that the improvements to the machinery over those years have been minor, and any redesign virtually nonexistent. Perhaps the most significant repair was to separate the General Counsel from the decision-making side of the agency. This was a policy change, not intended to improve efficiency, though improved efficiency has been one of its results.

The delegation of decision-making authority to regional directors in representation cases was another repair and has been much touted as effecting a major improvement in the Board's procedures. But a close look at the data strongly suggests that its impact on promptness and efficiency has probably been much overrated. It has, however, been of some value in enabling the agency to cope with its ever-increasing case load.

Effective implementation of standards of timeliness and standards of performance have been accomplished primarily by sound administration from within rather than by any repair or redesign from without. The Congress has not had to tamper with the basic structure of the agency in order to make most of the General Counsel's operations efficient. That efficiency has been enforced by General Counsels dedicated to improving timeliness and productivity and who are assisted by career administrators who have followed through and implemented the intent of the presidentially appointed General Counsels.

In insisting that the Board employ no attorneys except as assistants to individual Board members, the Congress may well have done a good judicial deed; but in doing that deed, it also created an administrative problem. This external "repair" has encouraged each Board member to build his own little kingdom and has effectively deprived the chairman or any administrator on the decision-making side of the agency of any opportunity for centralized control of timeliness or performance on the "Board side" of the agency. Similarly, in enacting the Administrative Procedures Act, the Congress may also have done a good judicial deed, but that "repair," too, created an administrative hardship; for, at least as it has worked out in practice, the "judicial independence" conferred by that Act seems to have rendered the Board and the administrative staff of its Division of Judges virtually impotent in adopting and enforcing administrative controls over that first-line decision-making function.

In sum, external repair and redesign seem to have helped the General Counsel by making him independent and giving him authority to run his own show, but the external repairs to the Board side of the agency have probably, *in toto*, hurt, rather than helped, the administrative effectiveness of the decision-making side of the agency.

REORGANIZATION PLAN 5

The major piece of external redesign and repair which has been seriously proposed over the Board's forty-year history, but not accepted, was President Kennedy's so-called Plan 5, which would have enabled the Board to review more cursorily many of the decisions of its administrative law judges and to be selective about those to which it would give more thorough review. The plan was defeated in the Congress some years ago.

Whatever one may think of the merits of that proposal—and one's opinions on that score are likely to be shaped by one's opinions of the ability and judiciousness of the current corps of administrative law judges—the statistics demonstrate that it would have had a relatively minor effect in improving timeliness. When one looks at the entire time span from filing of charge to entry of enforceable court decision, one discovers that the Board's assembly line review process takes a median time of about 130 days, of which at least 30 days is dead waiting time while briefs are being filed and other mechanics of the appeal are taking place. This means the Board's actual decision-making time runs, on the median, slightly over three months. Even if a provision for more cursory review could cut this time in half, only about one and one-half to two months could be saved out of a total two-year process.

Although former Chairman Murphy once estimated that this Plan 5 variety of certiorari approach could save 180 days in case-processing time, one can find no rational basis for such a prediction. A maximum saving of from 45 to 60 days seems more in line with reality if one examines carefully the segments of time involved in processing cases. Thus, while in virtually every session of the Congress someone seeks to breathe life back into this previously defeated plan, it must be doubted whether such a change would have any major effect on the dispatch with which the Board exercises its decision-making function.

Former Chairman Murphy also appointed a task force of labor, management, and public members to review internal Board procedures and processes and to recommend improvements in efficiency and performance which would not require external repair or redesign. As was predictable, although the task force labored conscientiously and formulated some sixty-nine recommendations, most of which the Board has now adopted, none of them are going to effect any fundamental change or improvement in the operation of the system. They could not be expected to do so. Both the Board and the General Counsel have, over the years, given a good deal of attention to administrative matters, and no outside group was likely, particularly on the basis of a relatively short period of study, to hit upon previously undiscovered means of improvement. The changes will, in large part, affect neither timetables nor costs to any significant degree. A few are doomed to predictable failure, such as the recommendation that administrative law judges be "prodded" to increase their timeliness and to improve their productivity. We have pointed out why such "prodding" has not been and cannot really be effective within the present system. Thus, this recommended "jaw-boning" will probably be about as effective as some other jaw-boning which the federal government has attempted within the last decade or two.

THE LABOR REFORM ACT

Representative Frank Thompson of New Jersey has introduced legislation in the form of a bill called the Labor Reform Act of 1977 (H.R. 77),[1] allegedly intended to correct deficiencies in the operation of the Act which Congressman Thompson says he has discovered in the fourteen years he has served as chairman of the House Labor Subcommittee on Labor-Management Relations. As pointed out in the *Daily Labor Report* for January 6, 1977, this bill "is similar and consolidates several measures proposed during the last Congress by Thompson. . . ."[2]

Plan 5—Again

One of these warmed-over suggestions is yet another attempt to breathe life back into Reorganization Plan 5 in the same manner as had been embodied in H.R. 8110 in the 94th Congress, First Session, 1975. We have already pointed out how that plan would merely further accentuate the cursory nature of Board review and would not materially shorten the total time lapse between filing of a charge and entry of an enforceable court order.

Election Proceedings

Another portion of the Thompson bill is addressed to the Board's election processes. It would require that if disputes over the appropriate bargaining unit or the eligibility to vote of specific employees are not resolved after forty-five days following the filing of an election petition, the Board must nevertheless go ahead and conduct an election in the unit designated by the union. We have already pointed out that the Board's record in the conduct of elections is a very good one, and that timetables on the whole are very satisfactory. The Thompson proposal, while well-intended, would probably have the unfortunate effect of dragging out election proceedings. A challenge to a unit would, in many instances, take place only after the election, thus leaving the results of the election in doubt and increasing the number of

---

[1] H.R. 77, 95th Cong., 1st Sess. (1977).

[2] *Thompson Introduces Extensive Taft-Hartley Reform Measure*, Daily Labor Report, January 6, 1977, at A-11.

cases in which a rerun election would have to be held because some defect was found in the unit. The proposed procedure would have the surface appeal of having elections conducted quickly, but holding an election is of no real value to anyone, particularly the employees in the unit, if the result of the election has little likelihood of finality.

It would also seem reasonable that delays in the postelection procedures would be more likely, since the pressure which currently builds to get problems out of the way so that the election can be held would be materially reduced. The election would have already been held, and there would be no other clearly identifiable dramatic event to motivate the staff to meet time targets. Time targets artificially set without such visible real targets are more difficult to administer. The proposal thus seems addressed to a very small problem (those few cases in which prompt elections are not held today) and may have the opposite effect of creating substantial time delays in many election cases because it can open the door to postelection unit challenges which are not now possible.

Encouragement of Maneuvers for Delay

The proposal presents a further problem. Although designed to prevent game playing for delay, it may well encourage just such game playing. An employer or union today will agree to a unit description so long as it can obtain a date for an election which is suitable, and will enter into an agreement for an election and waive its rights to a hearing. The sophisticated practitioner knows that he can obtain somewhere between four and eight weeks if he agrees to an election, because the Board and the other parties know he can obtain about that much time if he raises issues and insists on a hearing. So, in most cases, an agreement is reached on that basis, and no hearings are necessary. Under Thompson's proposed legislation, there is no incentive for the parties to reach such an agreement. If they do not, the election will be held after at least forty-five days, and no party will have waived its right to a hearing. Thus, any experienced labor attorney—and there are over 8,000 of them now practicing—will, doubtless, advise his client *not* to agree to an election. The Board will hold the election anyway; and if either the employer or a nonpetitioning but interested union does not like how the election comes out, it can then demand a hearing and delay the certification until after the hearing and a Board decision. Because this will substantially increase the number of "R" case hearings, the Board's workload will enjoy an immediate bulge, and there will be delays resulting from the Board's inability to cope with that increase. The net result—further delay.

Card-Check Recognition

Thompson's bill would also permit certification of a union if at least 55 percent of the workers in an appropriate unit are shown to be members by card check. This is a highly controversial policy matter and is not really a procedural reform at all. It would represent a substantial and serious change in direction in the federal labor policy. In a discussion directed primarily at the administration of the law rather than at its substance, we would point out only that, because card-check recognition has been and is so highly charged with emotion, it is only reasonable to expect widespread contests of certifications if this provision were to become law. There would be endless litigation of the circumstances under which each card was signed, whether there was any fraud or misrepresentation involved, and so on. Imagine the length of a hearing in which the circumstances of the signing of each card in a thousand-person unit will be subject to examination and cross-examination of both the card signer and any witnesses to the signing! It is difficult to imagine a more successful means of clogging the Board's calendar and creating total administrative chaos.

Self-Enforcing Board Orders

The Thompson bill also attempts to make Board orders "self-enforcing," unless and until a court of appeals either sets them aside or orders, upon petition of the respondent, the order stayed pending determination of the appeal. This change could substantially affect the timetable for effectuating compliance with Board orders, if the courts of appeals are chary with respect to issuing stays. Court review time is, as we have pointed out earlier in this appraisal, a substantial delay factor. Thus, if the courts routinely refuse stays except in the most novel cases or those which appear at first blush to involve egregious Board error, it seems likely that there might indeed be quicker compliance. If respondents realize that court appeals are not likely to forestall the entry of an effective order, there may well be a reduction in the number of appeals.

On the other hand, if stays are regularly granted, these provisions would have little effect. The Board's enforcement attorneys are now getting to the courts of appeals promptly, so it makes little difference whether the review process is triggered, as now in most cases, by the Board's petition for enforcement or, as would be true under the Thompson bill, by the respondent's seeking review. The difference, therefore, lies in the stay or no-stay decision of the courts of appeals.

In deciding whether to grant stays routinely or charily, presumably the courts will take into account the fact that Board orders are set aside in only a small percentage of cases. On the other hand, each circuit—indeed, each judge—will have its own view of how reliable the Board is as a judiciary, both generally and at any given time. A court will also recognize that, in many cases, there will be no genuine way of unscrambling the eggs, so to speak, once it has required compliance with the Board's order. For example, if a discharged employee is ordered reinstated but later held not to have been entitled to reinstatement, how can the situation ever be restored to the *status quo ante?* What of the innocent employee who was hired to fill the place of the alleged discriminatee and who may have had to be fired to make room for the discharged employee whom the Board ordered reinstated? How can a bargaining order be retroactively cancelled if the court ultimately finds it was not warranted? A "bargain" may already have been made—will the court now really order it undone? Will at least some courts of appeals weigh these matters in the balance scale and be liberal with their stays? Or at least much more liberal than if the forum which had entered the order had been a federal district court—another arm of the federal judiciary?

For that matter, will the Congress be willing to grant such self-enforcing authority to a Board which has so often, rightly or wrongly, been accused of changing in its decisional attitudes as the political parties of administrations change? Might the Congress decide to give such self-enforcing authority only to decisions of a *real* judiciary and not to administrative quasi-judicial agencies in a field so fraught with partisan controversy as is the field of labor relations disputes?

Only time will tell whether this "self-enforcing" proposal can pass the Congress and whether, if enacted, the courts will be sufficiently chary with stays to effect any real change in enforcement timetables.

Section 10(j) Injunctions

H.R. 77 also seeks to encourage increased use of Section 10(j) injunctions by spelling out standards which must be applied by the NLRB in deciding whether to seek such injunctions and, presumably, by setting standards for the courts to use in determining whether to grant injunctions. The inclusion of such specific standards, in my judgment, may well increase, rather than decrease, delay; the question of whether the statutory standards have been met will, no doubt, be litigated in each case, thus requiring both the Board and the courts to address themselves to these additional issues rather than leaving such matters to administrative discretion, as is now the case. This will complicate the tasks of both the NLRB and the courts in these injunction matters. Although a well-intended reform, this change, like some of the others, seems likely to have exactly the opposite effect from the one intended.

Remedial Authority

Thompson also proposes to give the Board further remedial authority. These proposals again present questions of substance and federal policy, but their effect on Board proceedings will surely be to lengthen those proceedings. Under the Thompson proposal, the NLRB would now in many cases face additional issues—*i.e.*, whether to enter "make-whole" orders in refusal to bargain cases and Section 8(b)(2) cases and whether to order the withholding of federal contracts from employers who "engage in willful and flagrant unfair labor practices" or who engage in "a pattern or practice of unfair labor practices." [3] Inasmuch as those issues would be of vital importance to employers against whom they might be sought to be invoked, one can reasonably estimate that strong resistance would be encountered in all such cases, and that the resistance would produce extensive litigation both before the Board and the courts. The net result would thus be to increase litigation and to clog both the Board's and the courts' calendars, with an all too predictable result of increasing time delays at all stages.

Board Appointments

The Thompson bill also contains some provisions relating to Board appointments which would require a Board member whose term had expired to continue to serve until a successor had been

---

[3] *Id.* at A-12.

appointed. That would, of course, permit the Congress, by delaying any new appointment, to retain a Board member whose term
had expired. Considerations of partisanship would therefore un-
questionably tempt the Congress to move slowly on approval of
appointments made by an administration of a party not dominant
in Congress; thus, the provision holds the danger of increased
politicization of Board appointments.

Limiting the General Counsel

The most administratively dangerous part of the Thompson
bill, however, is its provision limiting the authority of the General Counsel to decide whether a complaint should be issued. The
bill would require the issuance of a complaint in all cases unless
an investigation discloses "no genuine issue of material fact" and
that "the charge involved fails to state an unfair labor practice." [4] This would presumably open up to mandamus proceedings
a failure by the General Counsel to issue a complaint in any case
where the charging party wished to challenge the General Counsel's judgment of whether the above standards had been met. We
have already pointed out that the General Counsel now succeeds
in disposing of over 90 percent of the charges filed without resort
to litigation. Any enactment which limits his discretion in the
administrative processing of these charges would adversely affect
this record, would build in obstacles to the effective performance
of the General Counsel's prosecutorial duties, and would, as a
result, adversely and disastrously affect the total administration
of the Act.

Thus the Thompson bill, taken *in toto*, offers little in the way
of improved effectiveness of the Board as an administrative
agency and would in many respects complicate its proceedings,
limit its ability to administer the Act effectively, and reduce the
already inadequate thoroughness of Board review. Like so many
well-intended pieces of patchwork legislation, it has good ideals,
but contains so many practical pitfalls that it could well end up
impeding what it intends to expedite.

THE CARTER-REVISED BILL

At a White House briefing on July 19, 1977, the Carter Administration gave its blessings to a revised version of the Thompson

---

[4] H.R. 77, 95th Cong., 1st Sess. (1977).

bill which was introduced in the Congress on July 19 by Senators Williams and Javits and Representative Thompson.[5] This
new bill omits a number of the items which Representative
Thompson had included in his earlier bill. It abandons the recognition on a 55 percent card-check proposal, the proposal to spell
out standards for Section 10(j) injunctions, the proposal for
holdover terms for Board members, and the attempt to limit the
discretion of the General Counsel in screening out nonmeritorious
cases. It also revises the other Thompson proposals. The new
measure also includes certain substantive changes in the law,
which we will not discuss here.

As for administrative changes, the Carter-revised bill addresses
itself to the following major areas: (1) an attempt to impose
deadlines for the holding of elections, regardless of whether
there are pending unresolved disputed issues in the representation proceeding;[6] (2) mandatory injunctions under Section 10(1)
for Section 8(a)(3) cases involving the discharge of employees
during an organizational campaign or during a period after
an election, but prior to entering a first collective bargaining agreement;[7] (3) an expansion of the NLRB from five to
seven members, with seven-year terms;[8] (4) a provision for the
affirmance of an administrative law judge's decision in an unfair
labor practice case within thirty days upon the motion of the
prevailing party and under procedures to be established by rulemaking, said action requiring a quorum of only two Board members;[9] and (5) a revised version of so-called automatic enforcement of Board orders.[10]

Withdrawal of Federal Contracts

Some of the substantive changes would also have an effect upon
Board processes. The substantive provisions include, for example,
a revised version of the Thompson scheme to deprive employers

---

[5] H.R. 8410, S. 1883, 95th Cong., 2d Sess. (1977). After a few amendments
were added on the House floor, this bill passed the House by a vote of 257
to 163. The companion bill, S. 1883, is pending in the Senate at the time
of this writing.

[6] *Id.* at § 3.

[7] *Id.* at § 10(1).

[8] *Id.* at § 2(a).

[9] *Id.* at § 2(b)(2).

[10] *Id.* at § 3(D)(3).

of federal contracts if they are found guilty of willful violations of a Board order or a court order. As pointed out in the above analysis of the original Thompson bill, if such willful violations were alleged, there would undoubtedly be strong resistance by employers and lengthy litigation. Settlements of such cases would be rare indeed.

Make-Whole Remedies

Similarly, the bill contains a provision for a remedy in certain refusal to bargain cases which would involve a so-called make-whole remedy. The remedy specified in the Carter revision of the Thompson bill provides that the make-whole remedy shall be measured by prevailing changes in wages and benefits during the alleged wrongful delay as measured by the Bureau of Labor Statistics in its *Average Wage and Benefit Settlements, Quarterly Report of Major Collective Bargaining Settlements.* The introduction of this definitive measuring stick, rather than a measure to be determined by the Board of what benefits might have prevailed had the legally required bargaining taken place, adds less of an administrative burden to the Board's work than the former proposals. (It will also presumably be attacked as being arbitrary, but we are not concerning ourselves here with the substance of the proposal.) This part of the bill is also limited to those cases in which the unlawful refusal to bargain occurs prior to the entry into the first collective bargaining contract between an employer and a newly selected representative, thus reducing somewhat its potential impact on the Board's workload.

On the other hand, because the bill leaves up to the Board the question of whether such a remedy shall be provided in any given case, it would undoubtedly stimulate substantially more litigation in Section 8(a)(5) cases. The General Counsel would be reluctant not to include a demand for such a remedy in his complaint in any pre-first contract case and, presumably, would be reluctant to settle any such case unless the settlement included such a make-whole remedy. Under present law, an employer who wishes, for example, to test the appropriateness of a bargaining unit which he believes to have been erroneously determined by the Board has only this route available—*i.e.,* a pre-first contract refusal to bargain in an effort to persuade either the Board or the court of appeals that his bargaining unit contention was correct. Most such cases today are decided on motions for summary judgment and proceed very promptly through the Board's procedures. Under the new bill, this would, of course, not be likely. Any employer faced with this kind of a remedy—which he presumably would face in all such cases—would demand and, doubtless, be entitled to a full hearing, so that the Board might, upon all of the facts, evaluate whether such a remedy would or would not be appropriate. Although it is the belief of the administration that the inclusion of such a make-whole remedy may deter employers in refusing to bargain, it remains to be seen whether the reduction in the Board's cases achieved by compliance inspired by fear of this monetary remedy would offset the increase in the workload of both the Board and the General Counsel which would be involved in the increased litigation and reduced settlements in Section 8(a)(5) cases which the provision seems likely to produce.

Section 8(a)(3) Violations

The proposal also requires double damage reimbursement for employees discharged in violation of Section 8(a)(3) (discharge during an organizational campaign or prior to a first collective bargaining contract). This, again, would predictably reduce the percentage of settlements in Section 8(a)(3) cases because the bill would make it worthwhile for employers to try cases which they currently might well settle in order to avoid litigation costs. The theory of this substantive part of the bill is, again, that it can provide a deterrent to unlawful employer action. It is doubtful, however, that very many employers deliberately fire employees in violation of Section 8(a)(3). Those few who do would, in all probability, decide that it is well worth the cost to continue to do so, but would take more pains to conceal their unlawful attempts and would engage the best counsel available to contest such cases as long and vigorously as possible. Those situations, however, are few and far between. The typical Section 8(a)(3) case is one in which there is a sharp contest over the true reason for the discharge. When a supervisor has, on his own, fired a prounion employee either out of deliberate malice or in stupid defiance of the law, there is usually very prompt settlement by top management when charges are filed and when it is made aware of the situation. Even a substantial number of borderline cases are settled when the employer concludes that, even though his heart is pure, the situation may look bad, that there is a chance of being found guilty, and that the cost of litigation well may exceed the cost of settlement. The cases which are tried are, by and large, those in which there are genuine credibility issues and differences about the reasons for the discharge. Even a very substantial number of those are settled today because the cost of litigation in many instances exceeds the potential backpay liability—particularly at the time of settlement. If double damages were required, there would be both an emotional and a calculated decision by many more employers to litigate. This would, predictably, reduce the General Counsel's settlement rate. If this settlement rate in Section 8(a)(3) cases were to go down even a few percentage points, the resulting increase in the trial calendar would be astounding, and it could reasonably be expected that the Board's calendar would soon become sufficiently clogged to affect current timetables very drastically and adversely.

If, of course, the above analysis is in error, and the double damage provision actually were to deter violations of the Act, then the flooding of the Board's docket would not occur. Congress will have to judge whether it is willing to take that gamble. Historically, the General Counsel and the Board chairman and members have not testified in Congress on such matters of substance. That has generally been the policy in order that those charged with the duty impartially to administer the Act not take partisan positions on controversial statutory proposals. Yet here is a situation in which a controversial substantive proposal may have a very real effect upon Board processes. It is also a situation in which one's policy judgment about the probable effect of a substantive change is hopelessly intertwined with procedural considerations. Congress has heard Chairman Fanning testify in support of the bill's objective, but it has not received, and probably will not receive, a full and frank view from the full Board, from the General Counsel, or from informed regional office personnel (who know more about the real world of Board operations than anyone in Washington) on the potential administrative consequences of this proposal. The absence of truly informed testimony could lead the Congress to take a gamble which may easily have precisely the opposite result from that intended—*i.e.*, it may cause a severe slowdown of the Board's processes.

Administrative Changes

Turning to the procedural or administrative changes, as such, my comments will not be substantially different from those made with respect to the original Thompson bill because the refinements made by the Carter changes do not, in most instances, alter the basic effect of the old Thompson proposals.

Election Proceedings. The attempts to provide definitive time limits for the conduct of elections contain some interestingly innovative provisions designed to force the Board into rulemaking on at least some issues involving the appropriateness of bargaining units. Thus, the new proposals provide that an election must be held within fifteen days [11] if the election petition specifies a unit which has been established as appropriate under a Board rule or under a decision in the applicable industry.[12] Since very few cases are ever absolutely identical, "decisions in the applicable industry" are not likely to provide a workable standard. Instead, and this is doubtlessly what the authors of the bill have in mind, the Board may be forced to establish rules defining appropriate units in certain industries and to establish standards as certain as possible. For example, the Board now has a rule of decision indicating that a production and maintenance unit in a single plant is presumptively appropriate. The bill would seem to have in mind that the Board would incorporate such a presumption in a rule. Thus, any petition seeking a production and maintenance unit in a single plant would be scheduled for an election within fifteen days, with any contests about the unit to be deferred until after the election. Where such a rule or applicable decision is not in effect, the election must be directed within forty-five days [13] or, in exceptionally novel or complex cases, within seventy-five days.

These rather innovative suggestions are designed to eliminate unnecessary litigation and to permit the holding of prompt elections. As pointed out in the analysis of the less refined, earlier Thompson bill, the result of deferring unit questions until after the election would inevitably reduce substantially the number of agreements in which the parties agree to the appropriate unit and to other details regarding the election. The employer who wants thirty or forty days in which to campaign is clearly not going to enter into a consent agreement when he knows that, agreement or no agreement, the Board is going to hold the elec-

---

[11] Increased to twenty-five days by amendment on the floor of the House. H.R. 8410, 95th Cong., 2d Sess., 123 Cong. Rec. H10666-67 (daily ed. October 5, 1977).

[12] H.R. 8410, S. 1883 at § 5.

[13] Increased to fifty days by amendment on the floor of the House. 123 Cong. Rec. H10666-67 (daily ed. October 5, 1977).

tion within fifteen days. He is not likely to deem himself ready for the election at that time, and therefore he will preserve every possible objection that he had, refuse to enter into any agreement, and litigate the matter after the election has been held, at least if the union should win. Since the certification cannot issue until any unresolved disputes have been decided, the only difference between these procedures and the ones currently in effect is that the legal disputes and lengthy litigation will now take place after the election instead of before and will take place more frequently because there will be a disincentive to entering into a preelection agreement.

Take, for example, a situation in which the petition covers the typical production and maintenance unit in a single plant. There are always potential unit questions. For example, in most plants there will be leadmen. Whether those leadmen belong in or out of the unit is an issue commonly worked out today by agreement. But the employer who is not willing to be bound by an election conducted in fifteen days, because he has had no adequate opportunity to make his views known to the employees before the election takes place, will refuse to sign any election agreement and will state his position as being that the unit placement of the leadmen requires a Board decision. Now, if the union wins the election, he will demand a hearing on this issue. If he and thousands of other employers around the country adopt this kind of course of action, the hearing schedule of the National Labor Relations Board would become clogged, and all cases, both representation and unfair labor practice cases, would be substantially delayed.

Elections would go right along, but the recognition issues which they are intended to determine would remain unresolved, in this author's view, for substantially longer periods than at present. The kinds of issues which could be raised would include substantial, less substantial, and frivolous ones. But the result would be the same. The legislation will not cure the ill which it is designed to correct. Indeed, it will spoil a substantial number of election agreements in cases where the problem at which the legislation is purportedly aimed simply does not exist.

The average timetable today for agreed upon elections is a good one. The result of what this author believes to be ill-founded complaints about those timetables will be, if this bill is enacted, the traditional reaping of a whirlwind. By utilizing a false premise, they will have secured misguided legislation, and the result may well be administrative confusion, chaos, and delay.

Seeking Section 10(1) Relief. The other deadlines which the legislation seeks to impose by fiat suffer from exactly the same effect, and the net result of all of them may well be far from the result which the legislation seeks to achieve.

The proposed requirement that the Board seek Section 10(1) relief for alleged Section 8(a)(3) violations occurring during an organizational campaign or during a period after an election but prior to the first collective bargaining agreement would likewise result in clogging the Board machinery, at least in its initial stages. The Board's regional offices are simply not equipped to deal with this number of court actions. Most of the alleged Section 8(a)(3) violations do occur during organizational campaigns or during the period after an election and prior to a first collective bargaining contract. Once a contract is entered into, the contract contains grievance machinery pursuant to which discharges can be submitted through the grievance procedure to arbitration. Even though the current Board does not subscribe to the *Collyer* doctrine of deferral to such grievance machinery,[14] the fact is that parties do not often resort to Board processes when these generally quicker and more knowledgeable arbitration tribunals are available. But during an organizational campaign and prior to the time a contract is entered into, if an employee is discharged, the union has almost no alternative but to support him and file charges with the Board, whether meritorious or not. To require the Board now to seek injunctive relief in any of those cases in which it finds sufficient merit to issue a complaint would very nearly double the unfair labor practice case load of the regional offices. Those regional offices would not only have to prepare the case for presentation before an administrative law judge, but would also have to prepare it for presentation in court and would have to deal with the problems of court deadlines, hearing schedules, court calls, and the like. The result would be a substantially larger administrative case load.

Although there is a good deal to be said for the equities of seeking prompt, effective action against illegal discharges of this kind, the dual-forum—court and administrative law judge—approach is one full of administrative headaches. If, in the long run, the American people and their representatives in Congress were willing to give the Board enough budget to handle this dual-forum litigation, the administrative problem could be licked. But

---

[14] Collyer Insulated Wire, 192 N.L.R.B. 837 (1971).

in the first year or two, it would not be; and it is entirely possible that, with this and the other increased administrative burdens which would result from the passage of the Carter revision of the Thompson bill, the machinery of the Board would be slowed very nearly to a standstill. It is difficult to recover from that kind of an administrative setback. Thus, even if sufficient monies were made available in subsequent years, whether the General Counsel and the Board could ever again catch up with their case load would be problematical.

Expanding the Board Membership. The expansion of the Board from five to seven members, with seven year terms, would not have any substantial effect on timetables. It would mean that cases will receive some additional attention from presidentially appointed Board members because each Board member will have a somewhat lesser case load. That is a desirable result. It would also mean that novel or difficult issues would take longer to resolve, simply because it is harder to reach a consensus among seven than among five individuals. It would also create seven, instead of five, administrative fiefdoms, since it does not propose to centralize administrative authority. The total impact of this increase in membership might or might not be sufficient to make any major additional delay in time schedules.

THE RISKS OF THE THOMPSON BILL
AND CARTER REVISION

The difficulty with both the old Thompson bill and the Carter-revised Thompson bill is that they do not start with a realistic appraisal of the specific areas in which the problems lie. Such a realistic approach, at least as this author views it, would lead inescapably to the conclusion that the Board's election machinery works well, is rather carefully tuned machinery, and ought not to be tampered with in any significant way, lest the changes result in jamming the machine. A study of the exercise of the General Counsel's prosecutorial and settlement functions demonstrates that this segment, too, of the agency structure works well, that it has been greatly improved through the efforts of many able General Counsels and their staffs, and that no amendment to the law should be enacted which carries a risk of creating a lesser settlement rate or which might lessen the General Counsel's ability to continue his remarkable settlement record.

The Risk to Election Proceedings

Unfortunately, both the old Thompson bill and the Carter-revised Thompson bill do contain features which seem likely to jam the election machinery and to throw a monkey wrench into the smoothly functioning settlement mechanisms.

As for elections, both bills would, in this author's view, result in significantly fewer voluntary preelection agreements and significantly increase the amount of litigation over the appropriateness of bargaining units. Elections would indeed be held quickly, but there would be a longer road to final resolution of the representation questions and to effective bargaining in those cases where a majority of employees choose to be represented by a union. Together with other litigation-producing aspects of the proposed legislation, these changes could result in the short term in so great an overloading of regional office staffs that a huge backlog of both representation and unfair labor practice cases would develop, thus slowing down all of the Board's processes. In the long run, if the appropriations committees were willing to increase the Board's budget substantially, this additional workload could, of course, be handled. The decrease in voluntary election agreements and the increase in representation case litigation, however, would not be a healthy change in what has been, by and large, the most successful area of Board administration and the area most free of litigation. A few "horror story" cases should not be allowed to bring about this kind of change.

The Risk to Unfair Labor Practice Proceedings

The proposed legislation also holds a risk of a litigation explosion in the unfair labor practice area. The risk arises from the bill's proposal to litigate Section 8(a)(3) discharges in two forums and from the litigious resistance which can be expected to claims of double damages on behalf of discriminatees, claims for make-whole remedies in refusal to bargain situations, and claims for possible loss of government contract remedies. The settlement rate would seem doomed to a serious decline, and the risk is one of an inundation of the NLRB paralleling that which has rendered the EEOC an almost totally ineffective agency.

A careful study shows that the real problems in effective administration of the law arise during the period between the issuance of a complaint by the General Counsel and the time at which an enforceable order is entered. The decision-making side of the

agency does not work well. The selection procedures for its initial
decision makers are unwieldy and tend to result in inbreeding
and in the selection of aging bureaucrats whose judicial competence is suspected by the Bar and whose freedom from administrative control has been virtually guaranteed by the Administrative Procedures Act and by a history which seems to have
produced attitudes of resistance to administrative attempts to
improve timeliness and productivity. Even so, the timeliness record from filing of charge through decision by an administrative
law judge may be regarded as tolerable. If an enforceable order
could be issued at the close of the trial, or within a reasonable
time after the actual trial, the law enforcement schedule would be
at least reasonably satisfactory.

The total median time lapse from the filing of a charge to the
issuance of a first-step decision (now rendered by an administrative law judge) is less than six months. If, by better selection
procedures and better administration, the timeliness of the judges'
decision making could be improved somewhat so that decisions
could issue in something less than the current median of over
two months' time, effective remedial action could come within
three or four months from the date on which the alleged law
violation was first brought to the attention of the public prosecutor. That would be justice rendered as promptly as has been
rendered anywhere I know of in our society.

TACKLING THE REAL PROBLEM AREA

All this suggests that the real problem area is with the procedures which now follow the initial trial decisions. As the
process is now designed, there are, it will be recalled, two appeal
processes which lie between the entry of the trial judge's decision
and the entry of an enforceable court order. The relevant question, therefore, is whether these two time-consuming appeal
stages which now eat up approximately eighteen months ought
to precede, as they now do, the issuance of an enforceable order.

There are at least two reasons why that question, in my view,
must be answered no. First, the initial appellate review now performed by the Board is all too cursory because of the impossible
demands made on the members' time by the huge volume of cases.
That problem will not go away, because that volume of cases
keeps increasing each year. The result is that, to keep up with
the tide of cases, there is extensive participation in decision mak-

ing by Board staffs. This staff participation, too, can reasonably be expected to be increased still further as case volume continues to increase. The Board has not coped well with efficient staff utilization and is not likely to do so in the future. Committees simply are never very good administrators, and the statutorily guaranteed independence of each individual Board member and his staff adds to the administrative problems.

The second reason why this two-stage appeal process should not precede the issuance of an enforcement order is the awkwardness of requiring a court of appeals to be the court which first enters an enforceable order. The entry of a first judicial order, it seems to me, should clearly lie in a trial court rather than in an appellate court. Furthermore, the unenforceability of the Board's order serves as an incentive for any respondent—company or union—to insist on appellate court review even though the chances of prevailing before the court may be slight. This not only adds to the delay in law enforcement, but clutters the dockets of our courts of appeals with routine cases which do not belong there.

There is, therefore, real justification for a reform and streamlining of this wasteful and ineffective multistep process. The first adjudicative step in the administrative process ought to be made effective, as it is in virtually every other kind of civil or criminal litigation. The first step, of course, must also be judicious in the sense of providing acceptable due process for respondents.

The Thompson and Carter Solutions

The old Thompson bill attempted to deal with this problem, as we have pointed out, by breathing life back into Reorganization Plan 5. We have already pointed out the deficiencies in that kind of approach. It also contained a so-called self-enforcing Board order procedure which would have posed serious problems for the courts of appeals in determining whether or not to grant stays in individual cases. The Carter revisions have attempted to deal with the problems inherent in these two approaches, and the newer bill does bring some fresh approaches to this segment of the time lag problem. It permits any two members of the Board to grant quick summary approval (within thirty days) of an administrative law judge's decision and further provides that, unless a respondent files a petition for review with the court within thirty days of the entry of the Board's order, the Board's

order is entitled to immediate enforcement upon petition therefor
by the Board.

Analysis of the Proposed Solutions

When looked at closely, however, it is readily discernible that
the summary two-member approval is not substantially different in concept from the old Plan 5, except that the new bill requires the Board to develop rules so that this can be accomplished
within thirty days after the law judge's decision. That may well
be an unrealistic time period. Presumably, any respondent is entitled to at least a reasonable time to brief the issues so that the
two Board members may at least see the rationale of any possible
defense, and it would seem that the General Counsel ought to
have some reasonable time to reply to the respondent's brief.
Ample time cannot really be provided for such briefing within
thirty days. Of course, in the process of congressional review,
this thirty-day allotment may be extended to sixty days, which
would be a more reasonable period; and, if the Board would
really act within sixty days after the law judge's decision, that
could be a significant time improvement.

Some due process, however, will have been forfeited in that,
even with the Board increased to seven members and even with
two-member panels performing this summary review process,
little real review can be presaged. The appellate case load of the
Board stands currently at over 1,000 cases per year. If those
1,000+ cases are to be given a preliminary screening by 3 or 4
two-member panels, or by 3 or more three-member panels with
overlapping membership, that would mean that each such panel
would have to screen at least 1 or 2 cases a day and to decide
whether the briefs of the parties seem to raise issues worthy of
review. If the Board members would do this review personally
and not seek to involve their staffs, it might be done with reasonable effectiveness. If an attempt is made to involve the staff in
the screening function, the additional layering of personnel would
make it infeasible. In either event, there would not be time for
any real review of the record at all, and thus any Board review
of possibly erroneous factual findings would be virtually nonexistent.

Thus, the new bill has inherent in it a high degree of confidence in the present corps of administrative law judges, a degree
of confidence which, at least thus far, has not been shared by the
attorneys representing either companies or unions. Those attor-

neys have virtually unanimously opposed the Plan 5 approach for exactly this reason. The Congress may, under pressure of doing something to improve the timeliness of Board procedures, override the unanimous views of these attorneys. That is, of course, the prerogative of Congress, but one may question whether, in attempting to improve the timetables, Congress should also not take a careful look at the acceptability of the judicial process it is going to approve. Congress must recognize that it is giving the congressional seal of approval to the Board's corps of administrative law judges and leaving very little real review by the Board of their findings in most cases.

Only in those presumably relatively few cases which the Board might find worthy of full review would there be any real study of the record and any thorough consideration of the findings of fact or conclusions of law of the administrative law judges. That poses some jurisprudential problems. But from the purely administrative standpoint, the congressional mandate of a two-member, thirty-day screening process could work and, if a more realistic timetable than thirty days is used, could force the Board to face up to quicker decision making—at the price, of course, of forcing the Board to make those decisions with scant attention to the factual record.

The attempt to shorten court review by the so-called self-enforcing orders is less likely to improve present timetables. Since the courts of appeals have such heavy dockets that they are taking nearly a year to process appeals, it would still presumably be worthwhile for any respondent who wishes to buy approximately a year's time to inspire his attorney to get on the ball and to put a petition for review on file within thirty days of the Board's order. It may be doubted, therefore, whether this provision would substantially reduce the court review time. If it did not, then the net time saved by the two-member screening process and the self-enforcing Board order would be perhaps sixty days. That two-month saving is not major if the approximately full year of court review time were to remain, as would appear likely.

Proponents of the Carter-revised bill presumably count heavily, however, on the mandatory Section 10(1) proceedings in bringing enforceable orders into a very heavy proportion of the Board's work—that is, the Section 8(a)(3) cases. Presumably they are also counting heavily on the deterrent function of the make-whole orders envisioned in refusal to bargain cases. We have already pointed out that it is questionable whether the make-whole order possibility would indeed deter violations or whether it would merely increase litigation. The mandatory use of the Section 10(1) procedure in Section 8(a)(3) cases would burden the district courts with substantial amounts of individual discharge litigation, which presumably they would not welcome and for which they are certainly not adequately staffed today. We have also pointed out that this provision would add substantial burdens to the Board's regional offices and would probably create serious administrative problems there. There could also be some injustices done, at least from the standpoint of respondents, in increasing the areas in which the courts could enter enforceable remedial orders merely on a showing that there is reasonable cause to believe that a violation of the Act has occurred—the test which is used in Section 10(j) and Section 10(1) cases.

The Need for a Specialized Labor Judiciary

One cannot help wonder why the Carter Administration did not choose to vest the federal district courts with the real trial function now being performed by the Board's administrative law judges instead of proposing to thrust this interim relief, reasonable-cause kind of determination upon those federal courts. In order to do so and to staff those courts adequately, there would of course have to be a recognition that an adequate number of judges specializing in labor law would have to be added to the bench. But if a substantial number of the Board's unfair labor practices are intended to be heard in a preliminary way in the district courts anyway, why not have them heard there all the way, and why not recognize that additional labor specialist judges are going to be required?

In short, the administrative area really requiring attention— the time lag between the time the General Counsel decides to issue a complaint and the time of an effective judicial order— could be much more efficiently attacked by frankly recognizing what the Carter-revised Thompson bill only partially recognizes, and which, indeed, it seeks to disguise. The truth is that the Carter-revised Thompson bill depends more and more upon the federal judiciary for effective enforcement of the Act and de-emphasizes very substantially the appellate role of the National Labor Relations Board, leaving it with what seems doomed to become an essentially rubber-stamp function in most of the cases.

This author, at least, would suggest that a more frank approach would be both more efficient and more acceptable. The decision making can and should be removed in unfair labor practice cases from the NLRB and placed within the framework of the federal judiciary. It is time to recognize the need for a specialized labor judiciary.

Such a specialized judiciary could be achieved through either more or less formal structures. There are those who have proposed a separately structured labor judiciary. Simpler, and perhaps more efficient because of greater flexibility, would be an assignment system within each federal district court which would permit the assignment of most or all employment dispute cases to a given judge or judges on a regular basis. A judiciary which was expert in the law and the practicalities of labor cases would be desirable from the standpoint of both efficiency and acceptability. It would also have to be recognized that some of the elaborate discovery procedures, which have operated to slow down much of our federal court litigation, would have to be streamlined and condensed in order to save time when applied to labor disputes.

But an acceptable, judicious set of first-line decision makers who would have power to enter a truly enforceable order would constitute an enormous improvement from the present wasteful and ineffective multistep process represented by the decision-making side of the National Labor Relations Board.

It has been proposed that the Congress ought to consider the impact on the judiciary of any new legislation it adopts. This would be very much to the point here. The Carter-revised Thompson proposal will impose a substantial additional case load on the federal district courts, but presumably no provision will be made for increasing the number of judges assigned to the federal district bench, nor will any special provision be made for insuring that there will be judges who are sufficiently knowledgeable in the field of labor law to deal promptly and intelligently with the kinds of cases proposed to be added in considerable quantity to the docket.

What this author proposes is that the problem be faced squarely, that the Congress deliberately plan to add to the federal bench an adequate number of qualified labor specialists, and that it place for complete litigation, rather than partial litigation, most or all of the unfair labor practice case load of the Board into the federal judiciary in the first instance.

If this were done, it would substantially reduce the volume of appeals. If the first decision were authoritative and could be stayed, pending appeal, only in unusual cases, as is the practice of the federal judiciary in equitable proceedings, the many cases which today are being appealed only for delay would, in most cases, not be appealed at all. The courts of appeals would not face the problem of how much weight they should give in deciding whether to grant stays of the decisions of a quasi-judicial agency. They would be faced with exactly the same situation with which they are faced in other equitable proceedings where the federal district judges are the first-line decision makers. The stay problem would be less serious, and the criticism of the system should also diminish, since there is considerably more respect at the Bar for federal district court judges than for the administrative decision makers produced by the federal bureaucracy.

CONCLUSIONS

This administrative appraisal of the NLRB shows rather conclusively that the regional offices of the agency, administered in large part under the able supervision of the General Counsel, are an administrative success. They handle a large volume of elections efficiently and without extravagance. They perform the public prosecutor function in a similarly effective and prompt manner, sorting out the wheat from chaff with a minimum of delay and with reasonably controlled staff sizes.

The decision-making side of the agency, however, leaves much to be desired in terms of administrative achievements. It has not matched the record of the General Counsel, not because individual Board chairmen and members and their administrative aides in the career service have not been able people or have not tried, but because, as experience has shown, the structure is awkward, and because legislative repairs have damaged, rather than helped, its basic administrative design. Its record is not horrendous, but it is spotty and far less impressive than that of the General Counsel.

Changes could be made by Congress which might improve the selection processes for administrative law judges and which could make that division more manageable. Legislative changes could also provide centralization in administrative management of the totality of the Board's decision-making apparatus. These changes would give the Board better tools for improving its record of judicial administration.

But even such changes would not cure the basic ills of a tentative, slow, three-step process. Fundamental redesign is necessary if significant improvements are to be expected.

None of the pending congressional proposals attack that basic problem, and many of them are patchwork proposals which may accentuate the ills of the present ill-designed structure and add elements of confusion and delay.

There *is* a need for improvement. If this appraisal can shed light on where the true problems are, it matters not at all to the author if the reader does not concur in the author's proposed solutions. We have had, however, too many scattershot proposals for solutions and too little definition of the target at which such proposals should be aimed. If this work can help to identify with some accuracy where the real problems lie and thus to narrow the area of debate about which solutions can best solve *those* problems, then this author will rest content. It was with that hope that this work was written.

APPENDIX

TABLE 1
*Percentage of Unfair Labor Practice Cases
in which Compliance with Board Decisions
was Obtained without Resort to Litigation
1965-1975*

Year	Percentage
1975	68.6
1974	64.2
1973	60.7
1972	56.8
1971	59.6
1970	58.2
1969	45.9
1968	47.8
1967	51.8
1966	43.6
1965	42.1

Source: Data obtained from NLRB ANNUAL REPORTS: *see, e.g.*, 39 NLRB ANN. REP. 210 (1974) ; 40 NLRB ANN. REP. 218 (1975).

TABLE 2
Valid Votes Cast in NLRB Elections

Fiscal Year	All Types	Elections Seeking Certification	Elections Seeking Decertification	Employer-Sought Elections	Elections for Authorization or Deauthorization of Union Security Clauses
1936	7,734	—	—	—	—
1937	164,135	—	—	—	—
1938	343,587	—	—	—	—
1939	177,215	—	—	—	—
1940	532,355	—	—	—	—
1941	729,915	—	—	—	—
1942	1,067,037	—	—	—	—
1943	1,126,501	—	—	—	—
1944	1,072,594	—	—	—	—
1945	893,758	—	—	—	—
1946	698,812	—	—	—	—
1947	805,474	—	—	—	—
1948	1,971,087	200,706	7,857	8,829	1,629,330
1949	2,004,418	476,181	17,078	30,817	1,471,092
1950	1,690,733	534,187	8,485	245,513	900,866
1951	1,928,628	574,401	5,350	13,059	1,335,683
1952	677,349	647,371	6,534	20,507	2,937
1953	650,796	629,806	8,947	9,933	2,710
1954	459,554	434,736	9,089	14,937	792
1955	466,809	416,911	11,825	36,531	1,542
1956	426,509	401,581	10,289	12,987	1,652
1957	421,544	394,773	10,156	15,846	769
1958	326,314	300,363	9,082	15,065	1,804
1959	401,421	355,529	14,656	30,265	971
1960	453,295	416,980	15,340	19,743	1,232
1961	421,428	390,461	16,604	12,849	1,514
1962	501,250	463,259	16,781	19,299	1,911
1963	456,519	423,302	11,648	18,667	2,902

TABLE 2 (Continued)

1964	501,064	468,961	12,419	17,612	2,072
1965	494,879	462,526	11,173	17,754	3,426
1966	538,238	498,845	9,393	26,216	3,784
1967	557,822	526,809	11,134	16,190	3,689
1968	509,538	462,646	13,784	30,342	2,766
1969	529,970	491,279	18,841	16,299	3,551
1970	537,773	502,489	18,000	10,913	6,371
1971	519,679	480,119	18,062	16,163	5,335
1972	524,013	489,332	18,040	12,105	4,536
1973	484,090	450,102	17,112	13,089	3,787
1974	489,209	449,758	21,269	11,387	6,795
1975	508,031	471,933	20,110	9,953	6,035
1976	422,635	383,601	24,887	9,859	4,288

Source: Data obtained from NLRB ANNUAL REPORTS: *see, e.g.*, 39 NLRB ANN. REP. 216 (1974) ; 38 NLRB ANN. REP. 225 (1973). The data for 1948 through 1951 include, in total valid votes cast, all types of elections, but no breakdown is shown here for the few elections run in each of those years in pre-Taft-Hartley directed elections. Thus, in those years, the total in column 2 will exceed the total of columns 3, 4, 5, and 6. Where dashes occur, data are not available.

TABLE 3

A Summary of the Total Workload of the Agency
1936-1976

Fiscal Year	Total Cases Filed	"R" Cases Filed	"R" Cases Closed	Elections Conducted	"C" Cases Filed	"C" Cases Closed	"C" Cases in Which Some Remedy Was Required	Cases Pending End of Year
1936	1,068	203	98	31	865	636	—	334
1937	4,068	1,173	571	265	2,895	1,751	—	2,080
1938	10,430	3,623	3,105	1,152	6,807	5,694	—	3,711
1939	6,904	2,286	2,339	746	4,618	4,230	903	4,046
1940	6,177	2,243	2,690	1,192	3,934	4,664	1,001	2,869
1941	9,151	4,334	3,698	2,568	4,817	4,698	1,187	3,624
1942	10,977	6,010	6,285	4,212	4,967	5,456	1,365	2,860
1943	9,544	6,141	5,928	4,153	3,403	3,854	1,110	2,622
1944	9,176	6,603	6,507	4,712	2,573	2,690	736	2,601
1945	9,738	7,311	6,790	4,919	2,427	2,312	576	3,237
1946	12,260	8,445	7,981	5,589	3,815	2,911	529	4,605
1947	14,909	10,667	10,442	6,920	4,232	4,014	658	5,058
1948	36,735 (Includes 26,099 UA Cases)[a]	7,038	6,817	21,277 (Includes 17,958 UA Elections)[a]	3,598	3,643	384	12,642

Year								
1949	25,874 (Includes 12,190 UA Cases)[a]	8,370	9,245	20,720 (Includes 15,074 UA Elections)[a]	5,314	4,664	853	5,722
1950	21,632 (Includes 6,544 UA Cases)[a]	9,729	8,761	11,322 (Includes 5,591 UA Elections)[a]	5,809	5,615	1,288	6,714
1951	22,298 (Includes 6,790 UA Cases)[a]	10,247	10,291	12,489 (Includes 5,964 UA Elections)[a]	5,261	5,503	1,204	6,375
1952	17,697	10,447	10,603	6,866	5,454	5,387	1,113	5,351
1953	14,756	9,243	9,909	6,208	5,469	5,868	1,232	4,289
1954	14,094	8,076	7,975	4,832	5,965	5,962	1,229	4,394
1955	13,391	7,165	6,171	4,392	7,165	7,442	980	4,114
1956	13,388	8,076	8,070	5,094	5,265	5,619	881	3,768
1957	13,356	7,797	7,514	4,888	5,506	5,144	1,064	4,416
1958	16,748	7,399	7,403	4,524	9,260	7,289	1,060	6,385
1959	21,633	9,347	8,840	5,660	12,239	11,465	1,529	7,663
1960	21,527	10,130	10,216	6,633	11,357	11,924	2,299	7,007
1961	22,691	10,508	10,242	6,610	12,132	12,116	2,709	7,293
1962	24,848	11,286	11,634	7,668	13,479	13,319	2,554	6,704
1963	25,371	11,116	10,981	7,141	14,166	13,605	2,468	7,397
1964	27,403	11,685	11,546	7,563	15,620	15,074	2,680	8,085
1965	28,025	11,989	11,797	7,824	15,800	15,219	2,688	8,911

TABLE 3 (Continued)

Fiscal Year	Total Cases Filed	"R" Cases Filed	"R" Cases Closed	Elections Conducted	"C" Cases Filed	"C" Cases Closed	"C" Cases in Which Some Remedy Was Required	Cases Pending End of Year
1966	28,993	12,620	12,487	8,392	15,933	15,587	2,766	9,400
1967	30,425	12,957	12,724	8,183	17,040	16,360	2,805	10,331
1968	30,705	12,307	12,409	8,317	17,816	17,777	2,861	10,286
1969	31,303	12,107	12,116	8,416	18,651	18,939	2,363	9,992
1970	33,581	12,077	12,000	8,437	21,038	19,851	2,996	11,220
1971	37,212	12,965	12,896	8,611	23,770	23,840	3,253	11,232
1972	41,039	13,711	13,438	9,226	26,852	25,555	3,488	12,797
1973	41,077	14,032	14,059	9,660	26,487	26,989	3,641	12,308
1974	42,373	14,082	13,542	9,112	27,726	27,016	3,958	13,581
1975	44,923	13,083	13,325	8,916	31,253	29,808	3,970	14,797
1976	49,335	14,189	13,184	8,749	34,509	32,406	4,191	17,996

Source: Data obtained from NLRB ANNUAL REPORTS: *see, e.g.,* 39 NLRB ANN. REP. 195, 202, 217 (1974); 38 NLRB ANN. REP. 203, 210, 226 (1973). While there may be some differences in method of reporting through the years, it is the author's belief that the data here are essentially accurate. "Cases in Which Some Remedy Was Required" includes all cases in which at least a notice posting was required. *See, e.g.,* 40 NLRB ANN. REP. 210 (1975). Where dashes occur, data are not available.

a During 1948-1951, unions were required to obtain authorization by means of an employee election before being entitled to bargain for a lawful union security clause. This statutory requirement was repealed effective October 22, 1951. Pub. L. No. 189, ch. 534, 82d Cong. 1st Sess.

TABLE 4
Median Days Elapsed by Major Stages—Fiscal Years 1950-1976
(Unfair Labor Practice and Representation Cases)

	Unfair Labor Practices					Representation					
Fiscal Year	Filing to Complaint	Complaint to Close of Hearing	Close of Hearing to ALJD	ALJD to Bd. Dec.	Filing to Board Decisions (Actual Decisions)	Filing to Notice of Hearing	Notice to Close of Hearing	Close of Hear. to Bd. Dec. and/or Dir.	Close of Hear. to Bd. Dec.	Filing to Decision (Actual Decisions) Reg. Dir.	Filing to Decision (Actual Decisions) Bd.
1950	220	36	79	144	—	41	15	55	—	—	—
1951	169	38	71	138	—	41	14	53	—	—	—
1952	160	41	68	178	—	26	14	50	—	—	—
1953	129	54	78	151	—	4	15	45	—	—	—
1954	65	52	73	135	—	3	17	51	—	—	—
1955	87	47	73	170	—	5	17	56	—	—	—
1956	105	46	61	154	—	6	17	52	—	—	—
1957	90	45	69	198	458	8	17	65	—	—	—
1958	116	43	74	234	467	11	17	54	—	—	—
1959	104	59	74	176	463	12	16	49	—	—	88
1960	52	66	88	149	426	9	15	54	—	—	87
1961	45	42	99	177	401	10	14	65	13	34	112
1962	47	47	67	153	367	10	13	114	18	44	153

Table 4 (Continued)

| | Unfair Labor Practices | | | | | Representation | | | | | |
| | | | | | | | | | | Filing to Decision (Actual Decisions) | |
Fiscal Year	Filing to Complaint	Complaint to Close of Hearing	Close of Hearing to ALJD	ALJD to Bd. Dec.	Filing to Board Decisions (Actual Decisions)	Filing to Notice of Hearing	Notice to Close of Hearing	Close of Hear. to Bd. Dec. and/or Dir.	Close of Hear. to Bd. Dec.	Reg. Dir.	Bd.
1963	49	55	71	119	326	9	13	108	17	44	180
1964	56	51	91	124	346	9	13	116	17	44	189
1965	59	67	123	122	390	8	13	107	17	44	182
1966	58	74	116	112	393	8	13	116	19	45	197
1967	61	65	101	128	389	9	13	135	20	46	215
1968	58	64	97	120	382	9	14	128	22	48	168
1969	58	59	84	123	368	9	14	138	22	49	233
1970	57	58	84	124	348	9	14	139	20	48	228
1971	59	62	80	141	370	10	14	152	23	50	239
1972	51	65	83	116	349	9	13	148	20	47	237
1973	51	58	76	133	356	9	13	147	20	46	241
1974	50	48	69	134	327	9	13	144	20	46	225
1975	54	55	72	134	332	9	14	137	22	48	246
1976	55	75	89	120	358	10	14	138	23	49	246

Source: Office of the Executive Secretary, NLRB. Where dashes occur, data are not available.

TABLE 5
Employment Statistics
(Professional Staff by Organizational Units)

Year	G. C. Headquarters	G. C. Regional Attorney	Field Exam.	ALJs Washington	ALJs S. F.	Board	Enf. Lit.	Exec. Sec.	Solicitor	Total
1975	50	517	467	59	20	114	94	7	5	1,336
1974	59	524	486	70	19	113	98	6	5	1,380
1973	56	508	475	74	20	112	94	7	4	1,350
1972	59	513	467	77	22	108	105	7	4	1,254
1971	34	474	386	75	20	109	125	8	3	1,234
1970	38	514	361	75	21	121	131	9	2	1,272
1969	41	526	361	84	20	130	131	10	2	1,305
1968	40	523	371	77	23	129	128	10	2	1,303
1967	39	495	373	78	21	121	116	10	2	1,255
1966	45	490	372	73	20	122	103	9	2	1,236
1965	38	478	346	65	16	124	101	8	2	1,178
1964	40	464	309	60	16	113	105	7	3	1,117
1963	45	460	298	63	10	115	102	5	2	1,100
1962[a]	41	427	256	60	11	118	100	6	2	1,021
1961	65	418	223	55	9	124	78	5	2	979

TABLE 5 (Continued)

Year	G. C. Headquarters	G. C. Regional Attorney	Field Exam.	ALJs Washington	ALJs S. F.	Board	Enf. Lit.	Exec. Sec.	Solicitor	Total
1960	63	386	206	57	9	106	74	4	2	907
1959	32	334	178	50	8	98	80	4	2	786
1958	31	190	176	38	8	77	50	4	2	576
1957	40	177	205	37	8	77	49	4	1	598
1956	37	159	226	37	8	80	49	4	1	601
1955	36	144	236	47	—	86	54	4	1	608
1954	22	155	247	47	—	92	83	4	2	652
1953	40	169	265	52	—	96	82	3	2	709
1952	31	146	237	49	—	69	54	2	2	590
1951	39	166	258	40	—	95	66	3	2	669

Source: Office of the Executive Secretary, NLRB. Where dashes occur, data are not available.
Note: 1962-1975 figures are average employment rounded.
1951-1961 figures are end of year employment.
a Office of Appeals transferred to Division of Litigation.

TABLE 6

Employment Statistics

(Nonprofessional Staff by Organizational Units)

Year	General Counsel [a]	Field	Enforcement	Administration [b]	Board [c]	Judges	Total
1975	34	588	49	252	70	47	1,040
1974	32	600	48	231	61	45	1,017
1973	33	597	47	232	68	41	1,018
1972	33	603	45	225	66	35	1,007
1971	25	536	51	212	62	32	918
1970	27	527	52	223	69	36	934
1969	28	561	56	239	69	39	992
1968	29	593	58	247	74	38	1,039
1967	29	587	52	232	72	36	1,008
1966	30	588	47	211	72	32	980
1965	28	542	49	195	72	32	918
1964	26	512	52	181	72	32	875
1963	31	510	51	186	74	30	882
1962	29	478	51	173	77	28	836
1961	36	458	43	184	82	30	833
1960	32	444	30	203	67	32	808
1959	18	397	23	177	52	22	689

TABLE 6 (Continued)

Year	General Counsel [a]	Field	Enforcement	Administration [b]	Board [c]	Judges	Total
1958	19	294	23	172	47	14	569
1957	18	306	19	151	45	13	574
1956	18	285	21	142	45	12	523
1955	16	303	26	137	47	12	541
1954	17	309	22	147	51	12	558
1953	21	356	28	170	46	15	636
1952	17	312	20	156	38	12	555
1951	25	428	23	199	43	15	733

Source: Office of the Executive Secretary, NLRB.
Note: 1962-1975 figures are average employment rounded.
       1951-1961 figures are end of year employment.
[a] Includes Operations-Management and Division of Advice.
[b] Includes Professionals in Division of Administration, who for this report are classified as Nonprofessionals.
[c] Includes Division of Information, Executive Secretary, and Solicitor clericals.

TABLE 7
*National Labor Relations Board
Personnel Compensation, 1935-1975*

Year	Professional Compensation [a]	Nonprofessional Compensation [b]	Total Compensation	Total Average Employment
1975	$35,769,080	$12,039,158	$47,808,238	2,426.4
1974	33,846,512	11,027,675	44,874,187	2,428.3
1973	31,669,263	10,148,351	41,817,614	2,388.4
1972	30,760,289	9,648,054	40,408,343	2,384.9
1971	27,210,954	8,529,205	35,740,159	2,167.6
1970	25,685,505	8,032,733	33,718,238	2,222.4
1969	22,663,973	7,402,545	30,066,518	2,314.4
1968	20,135,538	7,166,978	27,302,516	2,360.2
1967	18,740,502	6,781,756	25,522,258	2,283.2
1966	17,498,300	6,360,488	23,858,788	2,227.8
1965	15,992,800	5,900,005	21,892,805	2,104.0
1964	13,799,801	5,285,273	19,085,074	1,993.5
1963	12,541,354	5,077,174	17,618,528	1,990.2
1962	11,137,659	4,531,740	15,669,399	1,856.5
1961	10,511,333	4,174,740	14,686,073	1,761.0
1960	8,833,960	3,344,431	12,178,391	1,606.5
1959	7,525,013	2,894,695	10,419,708	1,352.5
1958	—	—	8,013,764	1,132.3
1957	—	—	7,558,341	1,129.5
1956	—	—	7,462,944	1,122.3
1955	—	—	7,247,986	1,174.6
1954	—	—	7,402,186	1,271.7
1953	—	—	7,327,754	1,293.3
1952	—	—	6,843,165	1,254.8
1951	—	—	6,634,004	1,384.6
1950	—	—	6,653,359	1,465.0
1949	—	—	6,538,918	1,537.8
1948	—	—	4,154,909	930.9

TABLE 7 (Continued)

Year	Professional Compensation [a]	Nonprofessional Compensation [b]	Total Compensation	Total Average Employment
1947	—	—	3,403,508	818.3
1946	—	—	3,151,519	831.9
1945	—	—	2,669,233 [c]	759.8
1944	—	—	2,462,034 [d]	713.4
1943	—	—	2,590,577 [e]	852.0
1942	—	—	2,244,360 [f]	778.7
1941	—	—	2,000,228	795.0
1940	—	—	2,265,823	865.0
1939	—	—	2,023,324	—
1938	—	—	1,574,339	—
1937	—	—	550,671	—
1936	—	—	486,221	—
1935	—	—	420,617	—

Source: Office of Executive Secretary, NLRB. Where dashes occur, data are not available.

Note: Compensation includes benefits, moving expenses, and special masters fees.

[a] Professional compensation includes all attorneys, field examiners, law judges, Board members, and professional staff in the Executive Secretary's office.
[b] Nonprofessional staff includes all clericals, administrative professionals, and the staff of the Division of Information and Security office.
[c] Includes $354,000 for National Defense.
[d] Includes $460,836 for National Defense.
[e] Includes $456,932 for National Defense.
[f] Includes $88,407 for National Defense.

TABLE 8

Staffing of Regional Offices
Number of Cases Handled and Time Lapse Statistics
1951-1975

Fiscal Year	Number of Cases Closed [a]	Number of Professional Employees in Regional Offices [b]	Average Number of Cases Per Regional Professional Staff Member [c]	Unfair Labor Practice Cases; Time Lapse From Filing of Charges to Issuance of Complaint [d]	Representation Cases; Time Lapse From Filing of Petition to Close of Hearing [e]	Representation Cases; Time Lapse From Hearing to Issuance of Regional Director's Decision [f]
1951	22,637	424	53	169	55	—
1952	18,721	383	49	160	40	—
1953	15,818	434	36	129	19	—
1954	13,989	402	35	65	20	—
1955	13,671	380	36	87	22	—
1956	13,734	385	36	105	23	—
1957	12,708	382	33	90	25	—
1958	14,779	366	40	116	28	—
1959	20,355	512	40	104	28	—
1960	22,183	592	37	52	24	—
1961	22,405	641	35	45	24	34
1962	25,027	683	37	47	23	44
1963	24,678	758	33	49	22	44

TABLE 8 (Continued)

Fiscal Year	Number of Cases Closed [a]	Number of Professional Employees in Regional Offices [b]	Average Number of Cases Per Regional Professional Staff Member [c]	Unfair Labor Practice Cases; Time Lapse From Filing of Charges to Issuance of Compliant [d]	Representation Cases; Time Lapse From Filing of Petition to Close of Hearing [e]	Representation Cases; Time Lapse From Hearing to Issuance of Regional Director's Decision [f]
1964	26,715	773	35	56	22	44
1965	27,199	824	33	59	21	44
1966	28,504	862	33	58	21	45
1967	29,494	868	34	61	22	46
1968	30,750	894	34	58	23	48
1969	31,597	887	36	58	23	49
1970	32,353	875	37	57	23	48
1971	37,200	860	43	59	24	50
1972	39,474	980	40	51	22	47
1973	41,566	983	42	51	22	46
1974	41,100	1,010	41	50	22	46
1975	43,707	984	44	54	23	48

[a] Data obtained from NLRB ANNUAL REPORTS: see, e.g., 39 NLRB ANN. REP. 195 (1974); 38 NLRB ANN. REP. 203 (1973).
[b] Data taken from Table 5, column 3 plus column 4.
[c] Column 4 derived by dividing column 2 by column 3.
[d] Data taken from Table 4, column 2.
[e] Data taken from Table 4, column 7 plus column 8.
[f] Data taken from Table 4, column 11. Where dashes occur, data are not available.

TABLE 9

*Data Regarding Productivity and Timeliness
of NLRB Administrative Law Judges
1951-1975*

Fiscal Year	Number of Administrative Law Judges Employed [a]	Number of Cases Decided by ALJs Decisions Issued [b]	Average Number of Cases Decided Per Judge [c]	Time Lapse Close of Hearing to Issuance of Judge's Decisions [d]
1951	40	624	16	71
1952	49	435	9	68
1953	52	530	10	78
1954	47	556	12	73
1955	47	416	9	73
1956	45	319	7	61
1957	45	370	8	69
1958	46	439	9	74
1959	58	762	13	74
1960	66	1,226	19	88
1961	64	1,056	17	99
1962	71	989	14	67
1963	73	1,085	15	71
1964	76	1,157	15	91
1965	81	1,290	16	123
1966	93	1,376	15	116
1967	99	1,491	15	101
1968	100	1,427	14	97
1969	104	1,363	13	84
1970	96	1,281	13	84
1971	95	1,367	14	80
1972	99	1,533	15	83

Table 9 (Continued)

Fiscal Year	Number of Administrative Law Judges Employed [a]	Number of Cases Decided by ALJs Decisions Issued [b]	Average Number of Cases Decided Per Judge [c]	Time Lapse Close of Hearing to Issuance of Judge's Decisions [d]
1973	94	1,543	16	76
1974	89	1,519	17	69
1975	79	1,299	16	72

[a] Data taken from Table 5, column 5 plus column 6.

[b] Data obtained from NLRB ANNUAL REPORTS: *see, e.g.*, 35 NLRB ANN. REP. 158 (1970) ; 30 NLRB ANN. REP. 164 (1960). These data probably overstate the actual number of written opinions, since it appears to count all cases, even though one decision may cover more than one case when a consolidation occurs. It is not possible to tell whether the data are consistently reported in that manner, since formal "action" is separated from "cases" in only a few of the reports.

[c] Average computed by dividing column 3 by column 2 and rounding to the nearest whole number.

[d] Data taken from Table 4, column 4.

TABLE 10

Number of Unfair Labor Practice Cases
Decided by ALJs and the NLRB
1936-1976

Fiscal Year	Cases Heard by Administrative Law Judges (formerly called trial examiners)	Cases Decided by Administrative Law Judges (trial examiners)	Total NLRB Unfair Labor Practice Decisions	Number of Contested Unfair Labor Practice Cases Decided by NLRB
1976	1,902	1,606	1,864	1,241
1975	1,512	1,299	1,756	1,703
1974	1,715	1,519	1,909	1,195
1973	1,762	1,543	1,972	1,258
1972	1,881	1,533	1,885	1,168
1971	1,589	1,367	1,681	1,067
1970	1,511	1,281	1,627	917
1969	1,491	1,363	1,553	1,108
1968	1,514	1,427	1,153	1,111
1967	1,592	1,491	1,603	1,198
1966	1,553	1,376	1,492	1,064
1965	1,491	1,290	1,374	974
1964	1,592	1,157	1,252	883
1963	1,155	1,085	1,067	905
1962	1,305	989	1,230	1,139
1961	1,047	1,056	885	766
1960	1,474	1,226	934	781
1959	1,158	762	531	475
1958	522	439	395	353
1957	550	370	265	248
1956	386	319	332	293
1955	404	416	461	415
1954	669	556	398	341
1953	612	530	584	526
1952	535	435	408	367
1951	670	624	498	419
1950	472	350	318	277
1949	314	328	342	298
1948	178	129	166	158
1947	328	296	143	143

TABLE 10 (Continued)

Fiscal Year	Cases Heard by Administrative Law Judges (formerly called trial examiners)	Cases Decided by Administrative Law Judges (trial examiners)	Total NLRB Unfair Labor Practice Decisions	Number of Contested Unfair Labor Practice Cases Decided by NLRB
1946	233	186	193	—a
1945	235	225	129	—
1944	219	185	139	—
1943	365	261	265	—
1942	282	201	180	—
1941	235	226	217	—
1940	255	189	398	—
1939	424	351	381	—
1938	723	418	187	—
1937	151	49	53	—
1936	145	69	61	—

Source: All data obtained from NLRB ANNUAL REPORTS in tables showing formal actions taken in NLRB cases, and also data in the chapters covering "Operations" during each of the years. *See, e.g.,* 34 NLRB ANN. REP. 200 (1969) ; 17 NLRB ANN. REP. 285 (1952). The statistics therein are reported in different ways during various periods of the Board's history, and differing numbers are even reported for the same year. For example, while the 1975 *Annual Report* shows 1512 completed ULP hearings in Table 3A, which is the figure used in this table, the *Report* at page 8 reports only 1075 ULP hearings as having been completed. The differences may well be between *cases* and *hearings*—i.e., when cases are consolidated for hearing, there will be more *cases* heard than *hearings* held. The same is true of Board decisions; this table reflects the number of *cases* decided, even though more than one case may be covered by only one decision where consolidation has occurred. But there are also irreconcilable differences. In the 1965 *Report,* for example, at page 21, it is stated that the Board decided 907 contested unfair labor practice cases. Yet Table 3A shows 974 contested initial ULP decisions. Thus, it is impossible to be sure that this table is completely accurate, but it will at least serve to indicate major trends. As a result, the author here has attempted to distill what appear to be consistently reported figures for computation purposes, but in some instances a different interpretation of the reports could have yielded somewhat different figures.

a During these years, the "Formal Action" table is not footnoted to show how many Board decisions adopted the trial examiners' reports and recommended orders in the absence of exceptions. Hence, the number of truly "contested" cases derived by the Board cannot accurately be determined.

TABLE 11
*Timeliness of Board Decisions in Unfair
Labor Practice Cases and Representation Cases
1946 and 1950-1976*

Fiscal Year	Time Lapse From ALJ Decision to NLRB Decision	Time Lapse In Representation Cases—Close of Hearing to Board Decision
1946	199 [a]	82 [a]
1950	144	55
1951	138	53
1952	178	50
1953	161 [b]	45
1954	135	51
1955	170	56
1956	154	52
1957	198	65
1958	234	54
1959	176	49
1960	149	54
1961	177	65
1962	153	114
1963	119	108
1964	124	116
1965	122	107
1966	112	116
1967	128	135
1968	120	128
1969	123	138
1970	124	139
1971	141	152
1972	116	148

TABLE 11 (Continued)

Fiscal Year	Time Lapse From ALJ Decision to NLRB Decision	Time Lapse In Representation Cases—Close of Hearing to Board Decision
1973	133	147
1974	134	144
1975	134	137
1976	120	138

Source: NLRB files, unless otherwise indicated. No data available for years not included.
a As reported in 18 NLRB ANN. REP. 2, 4 (1953).
b The 1953 NLRB ANNUAL REPORT shows this figure to be 161 days, but as having been reduced to 116 days by the second half of the fiscal year. 18 NLRB ANN. REP. 4 (1953).

TABLE 12
Comparative Chronological Data Regarding
Productivity of Board Members' Staffs
1951-1975

Fiscal Year	Contested Unfair Labor Practice Decisions	Contested Representation Decisions	Total ULP and Representation Decisions	Number of Professional Employees on Board Members' Staffs	Average Decisions Per Staff Member [a]
1951	295	1,609	1,904	95	20
1952	256	1,779	2,035	69	29
1953	383	2,195	2,578	96	27
1954	229	1,562	1,791	92	19
1955	314	1,669	1,983	86	23
1956	200	1,452	1,652	80	21
1957	154	1,410	1,564	77	20
1958	220	1,571	1,791	77	23
1959	286	1,794	2,080	98	21
1960	383	2,240	2,623	106	25
1961	415	2,213	2,628	124	21
1962	640	655	1,295	118	11
1963	611	203	814	115	7
1964	547	176	723	113	6
1965	745	182	927	124	7
1966	760	157	917	122	8
1967	803	173	976	121	8
1968	817	143	960	129	7
1969	813	127	940	130	7
1970	719	137	856	121	7
1971	836	140	976	109	9
1972	866	166	1,032	108	10
1973	963	122	1,085	112	10
1974	977	156	1,133	113	10
1975	855	185	1,040	114	9

Source: Office of the Executive Secretary, NLRB.
Note: As to contested unfair labor practices, the table refers to numbers of *decisions* issued. Since one decision may cover more than one case (when consolidations have occurred) these numbers will vary from the numbers of *cases* reported in other tables. As to representation cases, this data excludes decisions on objections and/or challenges and AC, UC, and UD decisions.
[a] Average computed by division of data in two preceding columns.

TABLE 13
NLRB Decisions in Contested Unfair Labor Practice Cases by Month and Quarter
1940-1976

Fiscal Year	July	Aug	Sep	Sub Total	%	Oct	Nov	Dec	Sub Total	%	Jan	Feb	Mar	Sub Total	%	April	May	June	Sub Total	%	Total
1940	—	—	16	—	—	41	32	31	104	—	31	27	49	107	—	23	28	21	72	—	—
1941	26	34	8	68	40.24	11	13	8	32	18.93	4	13	14	31	18.34	13	10	15	38	22.49	169
1942	13	36	11	60	34.68	11	10	15	36	20.81	12	11	11	34	19.65	12	12	19	43	24.86	173
1943	20	15	17	52	19.26	21	18	25	64	23.70	17	36	25	78	28.89	29	24	23	76	28.15	270
1944	21	13	9	43	29.45	14	10	11	35	23.97	13	10	9	32	21.92	3	18	15	36	24.66	146
1945	12	13	6	31	25.62	16	6	7	29	23.97	6	10	8	24	19.83	5	7	25	37	30.58	121
1946	9	15	7	31	16.85	18	9	10	37	20.11	13	18	21	52	28.26	31	15	18	64	34.78	184
1947	17	40	7	64	48.49	7	4	8	19	14.39	8	8	9	25	18.94	7	8	9	24	18.18	132
1948	9	16	—	25	—	—	—	11	22	—	16	14	15	45	—	11	12	11	34	—	126
1949	19	21	19	59	25.54	4	18	19	41	17.75	7	11	26	44	19.05	33	20	34	87	37.06	231
1950	11	12	16	39	18.14	18	14	30	62	28.84	7	16	22	45	20.93	20	19	30	69	32.09	215
1951	22	21	17	60	20.34	28	25	22	75	25.42	22	24	21	67	22.71	27	35	31	93	31.53	295
1952	36	23	16	75	29.30	22	18	27	67	26.17	16	14	17	47	18.36	12	17	38	67	26.17	256
1953	18	21	12	51	—	14	17	47	78	—	42	—	52	—	—	—	—	—	—	—	—
1954	24	34	2	60	—	7	16	21	44	—	18	20	15	53	—	26	21	—	71	—	—
1955	34	26	21	81	25.80	20	20	48	88	28.02	23	16	35	74	23.57	28	20	23	71	22.61	314
1956	19	41	5	65	32.50	31	19	17	67	33.50	10	15	12	37	18.50	11	10	10	31	15.50	200
1957	16	25	7	48	31.17	6	8	10	24	15.58	4	9	18	31	20.13	19	15	17	51	33.12	154

1958	20	15	10	45	20.46	17	12	24	53	24.09	9	21	12	42	19.09	23	27	30	80	36.36	220
1959	16	25	17	58	20.28	32	12	30	74	25.87	20	26	28	74	25.88	24	25	31	80	27.97	286
1960	14	31	17	62	16.19	20	33	47	100	26.11	27	38	38	103	26.89	44	32	42	118	30.81	383
1961	23	54	14	91	21.93	24	26	17	67	16.14	32	57	57	146	35.18	27	43	41	111	26.75	415
1962	28	57	33	118	18.43	82	66	64	212	33.13	58	48	60	166	25.94	57	34	53	144	22.50	640
1963	49	28	66	143	23.40	54	47	30	131	21.44	34	48	73	155	25.37	62	32	88	82	29.79	611
1964	34	43	43	120	21.94	25	44	37	106	19.38	43	43	29	115	21.02	52	54	100	206	37.66	547
1965	9	58	49	116	15.57	58	67	78	203	27.25	54	57	81	192	25.77	52	62	120	234	31.41	745
1966	61	53	64	178	23.42	36	66	55	157	20.66	46	28	80	154	20.26	63	52	156	271	35.66	760
1967	22	32	42	96	11.95	72	52	50	174	21.67	65	47	71	183	22.79	56	118	176	350	48.59	803
1968	27	43	40	110	13.46	56	62	46	164	20.07	64	74	85	223	27.30	91	85	144	320	39.17	817
1969	47	37	51	135	16.60	51	56	48	155	19.07	47	65	67	179	22.02	85	59	200	344	42.31	813
1970	8	35	44	87	12.10	49	33	75	157	21.83	57	49	62	168	23.37	60	76	171	307	42.70	719
1971	29	76	19	124	14.83	67	71	81	219	26.20	79	51	92	222	26.55	86	64	121	271	32.42	836
1972	62	79	59	200	23.10	65	54	58	177	20.44	88	51	68	207	23.90	86	82	114	282	32.56	866
1973	75	71	62	208	21.60	103	82	58	243	25.23	65	64	96	225	23.37	95	77	115	287	29.80	963
1974	64	107	42	213	21.80	69	97	52	218	22.31	92	60	77	229	23.44	70	77	170	317	32.45	977
1975	38	41	64	143	16.72	71	77	103	251	29.36	63	48	74	185	21.64	53	69	154	276	32.28	855
1976	94	54	108	256	24.78	86	74	50	210	20.33	84	70	77	231	22.36	75	61	200	336	32.53	1,033
1977	80	126	142	348	30.87	52	67	100	219	19.43	159	49	71	279	24.75	95	80	106	281	24.95	1,127

Source: Office of the Executive Secretary, NLRB. Dashes indicate an absence of data currently readily available.
Note: Percentages rounded to equal 100.

TABLE 14

*Summary of Allegations Acted on by ALJs and the Board
in Initial Contested ULP Decisions
(Published fiscal year 1972, 1973, and 1974)*

Allegations	1974 Number	1974 Percent	1973 Number	1973 Percent	1972 Number	1972 Percent
TOTAL ALLEGATIONS	1,294	100.0	1,353	100.0	1,179	100.0
8(a) (1)	396	30.6	437	32.0	334	28.0
(2)	31	2.4	38	3.0	36	3.0
(3)	371	28.7	427	32.0	326	28.0
(4)	22	1.7	28	2.0	23	2.0
(5)	221	17.1	226	17.0	204	17.0
8(b) (1) (A)	71	5.5	59	4.0	86	7.0
(1) (B)	20	1.5	19	1.5	27	2.0
(2)	61	4.7	60	4.0	63	5.0
(3)	12	0.9	7	1.0	22	2.0
(4) (A),(B),(C)	59	4.6	29	2.0	31	3.0
(4) (D)	3	0.2	3	0.2	6	1.0
(5)	1	0.1	0	—	1	—
(6)	1	0.1	—	—	—	—
(7) (A),(B),(C)	15	1.1	15	1.0	12	1.0
8(e)	10	0.8	5	0.3	8	1.0

Source: Office of the Executive Secretary, NLRB. Where dashes occur, no data is available.

TABLE 15

Analysis of Volume of Work of Enforcement Litigation Staff

Fiscal Year	Total Professionals Assigned to Enforcement Litigation[a]	Staff Years Allocated to Brief Writing (NLRB Productivity Data)[b]	Number of Briefs Filed[b]	Rate of Briefs per Staff Year (NLRB Productivity Data)[b]
1967	116	44.3	312	8.0
1968	128	50.3	344	6.8
1969	131	47.8	335	7.0
1970	131	48.7	323	6.6
1971	125	44.2	330	7.5
1972	105	45.2	371	8.2
1973	94	41.0	287	7.0
1974	98	42.8	269	6.3
1975	94	37.7	272	7.2
1976	100	40.5	325	8.0
1977	110	42.9	360	8.4

Note: Table 15 has been revised for the second edition based on additional data supplied by the General Counsel's Office, NLRB.

[a]Data taken from Table 5, column 8; totals include all professionals, even though they spent part of their time on Supreme Court matters, contempt proceedings, and miscellaneous litigation. All professionals in the General Counsel's Office of Appeals are also administratively included in this staff, even though they spent no time on appellate court cases.

[b]Data supplied by General Counsel's Office, NLRB, and are derived from data maintained by the agency for productivity measurement and budget purposes. They are derived from time recorded by each professional as being spent on main briefs in appellate cases, and include time spent drafting, supervising, and editing briefs, as well as a proportionate allocation of overhead time such as leaves, sickness, administrative items, and other nonproductive time. They thus exclude time spent on Supreme Court matters, contempt proceedings, and also effectively exclude time spent by the attorneys who work full time in the General Counsel's Office of Appeals.

TABLE 16
Summary Analysis of Cost Per Case

Fiscal Year	Number of Cases [a]	Total NLRB Obligations and Expenditures [b]	Average Cost Per Case [c]
1976	46,136	$68,513,806	$1,485
1975	43,707	62,452,479	1,429
1974	41,100	55,178,041	1,343
1973	41,566	49,864,567	1,200
1972	39,474	47,638,923	1,207
1971	37,200	41,540,935	1,117
1970	32,353	39,054,913	1,207
1965	27,199	25,721,156	946
1960	22,183	15,105,927	681
1954 [d]	13,989	8,786,226	628
1950	20,640	8,594,933	416
1943 [d]	9,777	3,598,992	368
1940	7,354	3,184,021	433
1936	738	620,571	841

[a] Total cases closed as reported in NLRB ANNUAL REPORTS: *see, e.g.,* 39 NLRB ANN. REP. 195 (1974); 38 NLRB ANN. REP. 203 (1973).
[b] Data obtained from fiscal statements in NLRB ANNUAL REPORTS: *see, e.g.,* 41 NLRB ANN. REP. 25 (1976); 15 NLRB ANN. REP. 218 (1950).
[c] Column 3 divided by column 2.
[d] 1943 and 1954 are used here because the 1944, 1948, and 1955 ANNUAL REPORTS do not appear to include fiscal statements.

TABLE 17

Reinstatement and Monetary Remedies to Employees
1939-1976

Fiscal Year	Number of Employees Offered Reinstatement	Number of Employees Receiving Backpay	Total Backpay For Year	Average Backpay Per Employee [a]
1939	59,398	3,063	$ 659,000	$ 215
1940	37,514	10,000	2,260,000	226
1941	47,902	5,181	924,761	178
1942	40,388	5,925	1,266,408	214
1943	8,361	5,115	2,284,593	447
1944	3,322	3,734	1,916,173	513
1945	2,044	1,973	997,270	505
1946	3,568	2,779	899,297	324
1947	5,078	2,656	1,105,000	416
1948	1,170	1,196	431,110	360
1949	1,458	1,994	605,940	304
1950	2,111	2,360	1,090,280	462
1951	3,864	7,630	2,219,980	291
1952	1,801	2,821	1,369,792	486
1953	1,754	3,186	1,357,180	426
1954	1,438	2,414	929,446	385
1955	1,275	2,024	881,220	435
1956	1,841	2,160	1,388,314	643
1957	922	1,679	601,059	358
1958	1,067	1,659	761,933	459
1959	42,078	1,895	900,110	475
1960	1,885	3,417	1,139,810	334
1961	2,507	7,147	1,508,900	211
1962	2,465	3,455	1,751,910	507
1963	3,478	6,890	2,677,511	389
1964	4,044	5,142	3,001,630	584
1965	5,875	4,644	2,782,360	599
1966	6,187	15,466	8,911,040	576

TABLE 17—Continued

Fiscal Year	Number of Employees Offered Reinstatement	Number of Employees Receiving Backpay	Total Backpay For Year	Average Backpay Per Employee [a]
1967	4,274	13,986	3,248,850	232
1968	3,107	6,274	3,189,340	508
1969	3,748	6,225	4,370,430	702
1970	3,779	6,828	2,748,781	403
1971	4,068	6,770	4,594,650	679
1972	3,555	6,225	6,448,640	1,036
1973	5,407	6,758	5,876,670	870
1974	4,778	7,041	8,445,840	1,200
1975	3,816	7,405	11,286,160	1,524
1976	4,440	7,238	11,635,885	1,608

Source: Data obtained from NLRB ANNUAL REPORTS: *see, e.g.*, 40 NLRB ANN. REP. 211 (1975); 5 NLRB ANN. REP. 36 (1941).
[a] Column 4 divided by column 3.

TABLE 18
Summary Analysis of Costs
Per Dollar of Backpay Reimbursement
1940-1976

Fiscal Year	NLRB Obligations and Expenditures [a]	Backpay Received By Employees [b]	Taxpayers' Cost Per Dollar of Backpay [c]
1940	$ 3,184,021	$ 2,260,000	$ 1.41
1943	3,598,992	2,284,593	1.58
1950	8,594,933	1,090,280	7.88
1954	8,786,226	929,446	9.45
1960	15,105,937	1,139,810	13.25
1965	25,721,156	2,782,360	9.24
1970	39,054,913	2,748,781	14.21
1971	41,540,935	4,594,650	9.04
1972	47,638,923	6,448,640	7.39
1973	49,864,567	5,876,670	8.49
1974	55,173,041	8,445,840	6.53
1975	62,452,479	11,286,160	5.53
1976	68,513,806	11,635,885	5.89

[a] Data obtained from fiscal statements in NLRB ANNUAL REPORTS: *see, e.g.,* 41 NLRB ANN. REP. 25 (1976) ; 4 NLRB ANN. REP. 158 (1940).
[b] Data obtained from NLRB ANNUAL REPORTS: *see, e.g.,* 19 NLRB ANN. REP. 8 (1954) ; 35 NLRB ANN. REP. 24 (1970).
[c] Column 2 divided by column 3.

Racial Policies of American Industry Series

Order from: Kraus Reprint Co., Route 100, Millwood, New York 10546

STUDIES OF NEGRO EMPLOYMENT

Order from the Industrial Research Unit
The Wharton School, University of Pennsylvania
Philadelphia, Pennsylvania 19104

* Order these books from University Microfilms, Inc., Attn: Books Editorial Department, 300 North Zeeb Road, Ann Arbor, Michigan 48106.

MULTINATIONAL INDUSTRIAL RELATIONS SERIES

1. *Case Studies of Multinational Bargaining and Prospects,* by Herbert R. Northrup, Richard L. Rowan, et al. (Reprint collection of thirteen published articles covering thirteen industries.) 1974-1978. $10.00
2. *The Reform of the Enterprise in France.* Official English Translation of the "Sudreau Report." 1975. $10.00
3. *German Codetermination Act of May 4, 1976, and Shop Constitution Law of January 15, 1972.* English Translation. 1976. $10.00
4. Latin American Studies

    (4a—Brazil). *The Political, Economic, and Labor Climate in Brazil,* by James L. Schlagheck. 1977. $12.00

    (4b—Mexico). *The Political, Economic, and Labor Climate in Mexico,* by James L. Schlagheck. 1977. $12.00

    (4c—Peru). *The Political, Economic, and Labor Climate in Peru,* by Nancy R. Johnson. 1978. $12.00

    (4d—Venezuela). *The Political, Economic, and Labor Climate in Venezuela,* by Cecelia M. Valente. 1978. $12.00

    (Future studies in this series will cover Colombia, Argentina, and Chile.)

OTHER COLLECTIVE BARGAINING STUDIES

Open Shop Construction, by Herbert R. Northrup and Howard G. Foster. Major Study No. 54. 1975. $15.00

Coalition Bargaining, by William N. Chernish. Major Study No. 45. 1969. $7.95

Restrictive Labor Practices in the Supermarket Industry, by Herbert R. Northrup and Gordon R. Storholm. Major Study No. 44. 1967. $7.50

INDUSTRY STUDIES

Prescription Drug Pricing in Independent and Chain Drugstores, by Jonathan P. Northrup. 1975. $5.95

Market Restraints in the Retail Drug Industry, by F. Marion Fletcher. Major Study No. 43. 1967. $10.00

The Carpet Industry: Present Status and Future Prospects, by Robert W. Kirk. Miscellaneous Report Series No. 17. 1970. $5.95

The Economics of Carpeting and Resilient Flooring: An Evaluation and Comparison, by George M. Parks. Major Study No. 41. 1966. $2.95

Order from the Industrial Research Unit
The Wharton School, University of Pennsylvania
Philadelphia, Pennsylvania 19104

MANPOWER AND HUMAN RESOURCES STUDIES

3. *Manpower in Homebuilding: A Preliminary Analysis*, by Howard G. Foster. 1974. $6.95

4. *The Impact of Government Manpower Programs*, by Charles R. Perry, Bernard E. Anderson, Richard L. Rowan, and Herbert R. Northrup. 1975. $18.50

5. *Manpower and Merger: The Impact of Merger Upon Personnel Policies in the Carpet and Furniture Industries*, by Steven S. Plice. 1976. $7.95

6. *The Opportunities Industrialization ⸗Centers: A Decade of Community-Based Manpower Services*, by Bernard E. Anderson. 1976. $7.95

7. *The Availability of Minorities and Women for Professional and Managerial Positions, 1970-1985*, by Stephen A. Schneider. 1977. $25.00

8. *The Objective Selection of Supervisors*, by Herbert R. Northrup, Ronald M. Cowin, Lawrence G. Vanden Plas, et al. 1978. $25.00

LABOR RELATIONS AND PUBLIC POLICY SERIES

3. *The NLRB and the Appropriate Bargaining Unit*, by John E. Abodeely. 1971. $5.95

4. *The NLRB and Secondary Boycotts*, by Ralph M. Dereshinsky. 1972. $5.95

5. *Collective Bargaining: Survival in the '70s?* Conference Proceedings. Edited by Richard L. Rowan. 1972. $8.50

6. *Welfare and Strikes: The Use of Public Funds to Support Strikers*, by Armand J. Thieblot, Jr., and Ronald M. Cowin. 1972. $6.95

8. *NLRB Regulation of Election Conduct*, by Robert E. Williams, Peter A. Janus, and Kenneth C. Huhn. 1974. $9.50

9. *NLRB and Management Decision Making*, by Robert A. Swift. 1974. $6.95

10. *The Davis-Bacon Act*, by Armand J. Thieblot, Jr. 1975. $6.95

11. *The Labor Relations Climate and Management Rights in Urban School Systems: The Case of Philadelphia*, by Charles R. Perry. 1974. $5.95

12. *NLRB Remedies for Unfair Labor Practices*, by Douglas S. McDowell and Kenneth C. Huhn. 1976. $9.50

13. *NLRB and Judicial Control of Union Discipline*, by Thomas J. Keeline. 1976. $6.95

14. *Old Age, Handicapped and Vietnam-Era Antidiscrimination Legislation*, by James P. Northrup. With 1978 supplement. 1977. $10.50

15. *Compulsory Unionism, the NLRB, and the Courts*, by Thomas R. Haggard. 1977. $9.50

16. *An Administrative Appraisal of the NLRB*, by Edward B. Miller. 1977. $8.95

17. *The Impact of OSHA: A Study of the Effects of the Occupational Safety and Health Act on Three Key Industries—Aerospace, Chemicals, and Textiles*, by Herbert R. Northrup, Richard L. Rowan, Charles R. Perry, et al. 1978. $15.00

18. *Fair Representation, the NLRB, and the Courts*, by Timothy J. Boyce. 1978. $8.95

Order from the Industrial Research Unit
The Wharton School, University of Pennsylvania
Philadelphia, Pennsylvania 19104